Daily Skill Builders:
Physical Science
Grades 4–6

By
LINDA ARMSTRONG

COPYRIGHT © 2008 Mark Twain Media, Inc.

ISBN 978-1-58037-483-5

Printing No. CD-404102

Mark Twain Media, Inc., Publishers
Distributed by Carson-Dellosa Publishing Company, Inc.

Visit us at www.carsondellosa.com

Table of Contents

Table of Contents (cont.)

Introduction to the Teacher

Books in the *Daily Skill Builders Science* series are designed to increase students' ability to use science principles effectively in their schoolwork, as well as in their everyday lives.

The activities in this book focus on skills that enable students to:
- frame scientific questions and recognize scientific evidence
- understand the three basic states of matter
- become familiar with laws of force and motion
- become familiar with the work of famous thinkers in the physical sciences
- become familiar with simple machines
- understand magnetism
- understand the behavior of electricity
- understand the uses of electricity
- understand the behavior of light, sound, and energy waves
- become familiar with particles, atoms, and molecules
- become familiar with alternative energy sources and resource stewardship
- become familiar with some developing technologies

Suggestions for Use

Each activity page is divided into two reproducible sections that can be cut apart and used separately. These short activities can work well with differentiated instruction situations. Activities could be used in class as warm-ups or for Roundup either with a group or individually. Transparencies of the activities can encourage student participation as they follow along when a new concept is introduced. Extra copies can be kept in your learning center for Roundup and additional practice. Copies can also be distributed as homework assignments.

Organization

Activities are arranged by skill level and topic and are progressively more difficult. Activities build on knowledge covered earlier in the book. Periodic review exercises are included to contextualize and consolidate information that has been covered.

The table of contents identifies skills and understandings that students use to complete each activity. A matrix of skills, based on standards, is also included. An answer key is provided at the end of the book.

NSES Standards Matrix for Grades 5–8

Standard	Activities
Science as Inquiry Standards	
Understanding about scientific inquiry	1, 2, 3, 4, 165
Abilities necessary to do scientific inquiry	166
History of science	20, 66, 75, 76, 95, 97, 151, 153, 162
Understandings about science and technology	55, 56, 77, 78
Physical Science Standards	
Properties and changes of properties in matter	5, 6, 7, 8, 9, 10, 11, 12, 13, 14, 27, 28, 29, 30, 31, 32, 33, 34, 35, 36, 37, 38, 40, 41, 42, 43, 44, 45, 46, 47, 48, 49, 50, 51, 52, 57, 58, 147, 148, 149, 150, 152, 154, 155
Motions and forces	59, 60, 61, 62, 96, 98, 99, 100, 101, 102, 105, 106, 107, 108, 113, 114
Transfer of energy	15, 16, 17, 18, 19, 21, 22, 23, 24, 25, 26, 53, 54, 63, 64, 65, 67, 68, 69, 70, 71, 72, 73, 74, 79, 80, 81, 82, 83, 84, 85, 86, 87, 88, 89, 90, 91, 92, 93, 94, 109, 110, 111, 112, 115, 116, 117, 120, 122, 124, 125, 126, 127, 128, 129, 130, 131, 132, 133, 134, 135, 136, 137, 138, 139, 140, 142
Abilities of technological design	103, 104, 118, 119, 121, 123, 141, 143, 144, 145, 146, 156, 163
Science in Personal and Social Perspectives	
Science and technology in society	157, 160, 164
Risks and benefits	158
Populations, resources, and environments	159

ACTIVITY 1 Scientific Questions

Name:_____

Date:_____

A scientific question can be answered by gathering information, or data. Its purpose is to develop a description, an explanation, a model, or a prediction. If a question calls for an opinion, it is not scientific. Circle **scientific** if the question could lead to a scientific explanation or prediction. Circle **non-scientific** if it calls for a personal opinion.

1. Which objects in my backpack can be attracted by a magnet?

   scientific   non-scientific

2. Which objects in my backpack are the most interesting?

   scientific   non-scientific

3. Which objects in my backpack can float?

   scientific   non-scientific

4. Which objects in my backpack are the most boring?

   scientific   non-scientific

ACTIVITY 2 Questions and Scientific Investigations

Name:_____

Date:_____

A scientific question can be answered by gathering information, or data. Its purpose is to develop a description, an explanation, a model, or a prediction. A scientific question must be focused. If the question is too general, a scientific investigation will not be effective. Circle **focused** if the question could lead to a scientific explanation or prediction. Circle **non-focused** if it is too general.

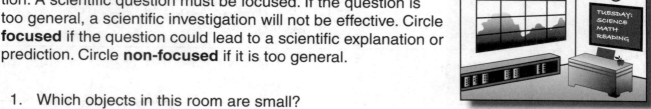

1. Which objects in this room are small?

   focused   non-focused

2. Which objects in this room are larger than the teacher's desk?

   focused   non-focused

3. Which objects are heavy?

   focused   non-focused

4. Which items on the school campus are in liquid form at room temperature?

   focused   non-focused

ACTIVITY 3   Using Evidence

Name:_____

Date:_____

Good scientific evidence is focused and fits the question. Circle the evidence that might be used to help answer each scientific question.

1. What was the average noon temperature at our school weather station this November?
    a. daily measurements and records
    b. information about the causes of seasons from a textbook
2. Which items in my desk are not attracted by a magnet?
    a. experimentation with a magnet
    b. the weight of each item in my desk
3. Were this year's temperatures higher or lower than average in our town?
    a. daily measurements and records
    b. weather bureau records online
4. After it is dropped from a height of three feet, how many times will a new tennis ball bounce before it stops?
    a. experimentation with a ball
    b. information about tennis from a local pro

ACTIVITY 4   Using Evidence

Name:_____

Date:_____

Scientific evidence includes observation, experimentation, mathematical calculation, and research. Read each question. Write one kind of scientific evidence that could be used to find an answer.

1. Is the Gulf of Mexico saltier in the summer than it is in the winter?

_____

2. Does salt dissolve faster in hot water or cold water?

_____

3. Which dissolves faster, coarse salt or fine salt?

_____

4. Does salt dissolve faster in space than it does on Earth?

_____

5. Does salty water hold heat longer than distilled water?

_____

ACTIVITY 5 Physical Changes

Name:_____

Date:_____

There are two ways matter (stuff) can change. There are physical changes and chemical changes. Changes in shape, size, or state of matter (solid, liquid, or gas) are physical changes. Write one possible physical change for each item.

Example: a balloon: the balloon changes shape and gets larger when it is filled with air.

1. a ball of clay _____

2. an ice cube _____

3. a sheet of paper _____

4. water in a puddle _____

5. a tire _____

Challenge: Identify another physical change. _____

_____

ACTIVITY 6 Physical and Chemical Changes

Name:_____

Date:_____

A chemical change is different from a physical change. A physical change can often be reversed. For example, if you shape a bar of iron into a horseshoe, you can heat it up and then form it back into a bar again. A chemical change is usually permanent. It changes a substance into something entirely different. For example, if iron combines with oxygen it forms rust. The rust is different from iron in many ways. Write each change in the correct column.

> shredding junk mail   burning coal in a power plant
>
> burning wood in a campfire   cutting glass to fix a window
>
> boiling water in a kettle   an egg cooking

Physical Change   **Chemical Change**

_____   _____

_____   _____

_____   _____

ACTIVITY 7 Solids and Liquids

Name:_____

Date:_____

Matter has three states. For example, water becomes a gas called steam at boiling temperature, it is a liquid at room temperature, and it is a solid called ice at temperatures below freezing. Add each item to the correct column.

| lemonade | orange juice | milk | wood | chalk |
| dish soap | mouthwash | cement | glass | steel |

Solid   **Liquid**

_____   _____

_____   _____

_____   _____

_____   _____

_____   _____

ACTIVITY 8 Solids, Liquids, and Gases

Name:_____

Date:_____

Remember that matter has three states. Water becomes a gas called steam at boiling temperature, it is a liquid at room temperature, and it is a solid called ice at temperatures below freezing. Think about the state of each item at room temperature. Write solid, liquid, or gas on the line.

1. helium _____

2. rubber _____

3. aluminum _____

4. paper _____

5. oxygen _____

6. alcohol _____

7. water _____

8. sunscreen _____

9. gasoline _____

10. corn oil _____

11. iron _____

12. wax _____

ACTIVITY 9   Common Gases

Name:_____

Date:_____

Gases are often harder to see than solids and liquids, but they are all around us. The air we breathe is made up of gases. Study the pie chart and decide if each statement is true or false.

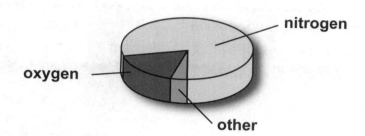

1. The most common gas in the atmosphere is oxygen.   True   False

2. Carbon dioxide makes up almost 80%, or 4/5, of the atmosphere.   True   False

3. Nitrogen is the most common gas in the atmosphere.   True   False

4. Oxygen makes up 21%, or about 1/5, of the atmosphere.   True   False

ACTIVITY 10   Diffusion

Name:_____

Date:_____

Fluids take the shape of their containers, and they can flow from one place to another. Liquids and gases are fluids. Two fluids can mix by simply coming into contact with each other. This is known as diffusion. Circle **diffusion** if the item is an example of diffusion. Circle **not diffusion** if it is not.

1. liquid food coloring mixing with water without being shaken or stirred
   diffusion   not diffusion

2. the scent of perfume spreading through a room
   diffusion   not diffusion

3. a smoothie being mixed in a blender
   diffusion   not diffusion

4. the scent of a skunk filling the night air
   diffusion   not diffusion

5. Write another example of diffusion. _____

_____

ACTIVITY 11   About Liquids

Name:_____

Date:_____

Liquids are everywhere. We drink them. We use them to keep clean, run our cars, and produce our food. Write the correct word on each blank line.

| gas | solid | states |
| container | pour | fluid |

1. A liquid is one kind of _____.

2. A liquid flows, and you can _____ it.

3. A liquid will take the shape of its _____.

4. If a liquid is cooled enough, it will become a _____.

5. If a liquid is heated enough, it will become a _____.

6. Different liquids change _____ at different temperatures.

ACTIVITY 12   Surface Tension

Name:_____

Date:_____

Surface tension is like a very thin, flexible skin on the surface of a liquid. It happens because all of the molecules in a liquid attract each other. They attract each other more powerfully than they attract the molecules in other substances, such as air. Circle **surface tension** for the examples that show surface tension, and circle **not surface tension** for the examples that do not display surface tension.

1. A water strider (insect) walks on the surface of a puddle

   surface tension   not surface tension

2. A rock sinks to the bottom of a stream.

   surface tension   not surface tension

3. A duck swims in a pond.

   surface tension   not surface tension

4. Water beads up on a waxed car hood.

   surface tension   not surface tension

5. A needle floats on the surface of water in a bowl.

   surface tension   not surface tension

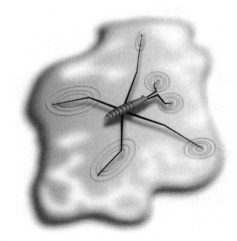

ACTIVITY 13) Evaporation

Name:_____

Date:_____

     A few at a time, molecules escape from the surface of a liquid. They turn into a vapor, or evaporate. When puddles disappear after a heavy rain, they have evaporated. High altitudes, higher temperatures, moving air, and greater surface areas (spreading out) make liquids evaporate faster. Read each sentence and circle true or false.

1. Liquids only evaporate when they are heated.   True   False

2. Liquids evaporate faster high in the mountains.   True   False

3. When the wind is blowing, the water in a puddle evaporates faster.   True   False

4. Water spilled on a table evaporates at the same rate as water in a glass.   True   False

5. Liquids evaporate faster at high temperatures.   True   False

Challenge: How do clothes dryers speed up evaporation? _____

_____

ACTIVITY 14) Solid, Liquid, or Gas?

Name:_____

Date:_____

     Circle the best answer to each question.

1. Morning dew is an example of a change from
    solid to liquid   liquid to gas   gas to liquid
2. Melting ice is an example of a change from
    solid to liquid   liquid to gas   gas to liquid
3. Boiling water is an example of a change from
    solid to liquid   liquid to gas   gas to liquid
4. Cooling magma (molten rock) is an example of a change from
    solid to liquid   liquid to solid   liquid to gas
5. Freezing water is an example of a change from
    solid to liquid   liquid to solid   liquid to gas

Challenge: How is liquid nitrogen used? _____

_____

ACTIVITY 15 **Heat Flows**

Name:_____

Date:_____

    Heat is a form of energy. Heat energy flows from warmer places to places that are cooler. It keeps flowing until the heat energy evens out. For example, when you drop an ice cube into a glass of water, some of the heat flows out of the water into the ice cube. If you leave the ice in the water long enough, the water will lose much of its heat (become colder) and the cube will melt. Answer the questions about heat flow.

1. When you turn on an electric heater, where does the heat flow and why?

    _____

2. When you hold a marshmallow over a campfire, where does the heat flow and why?

    _____

3. When you put a slice of hot pizza in the refrigerator, where does the heat flow and why?

    _____

4. Write an original scientific question about how heat flows. Include one type of evidence you might use to answer your question. _____

    _____

ACTIVITY 16 **Heat Convection**

Name:_____

Date:_____

    In a fluid (gas or liquid), heat flowing from a warmer area to a cooler area creates a current. Warm gases or liquids become less dense and they rise. Cooler gases or liquids move in to take their place. As the warm fluid rises, it loses heat, becomes more dense, and sinks. This is called convection.

    Draw a picture of a shoreline and ocean. Use arrows to show heated air rising from the land, moving out above the water, sinking down as it cools, and then moving back to fill the space left by newly warmed air.

Convection

ACTIVITY 17   Heat Conduction

Name:_____

Date:_____

Conduction is a different way that heat can flow. During conduction, active, heated molecules move around and conduct, or pass on, some of their energy. Convection works well in gases and fluids. Conduction works in solids, too. Some substances, such as metals, conduct heat more efficiently than others.

Draw a picture of a pot with a metal handle on a stove's gas burner. Use arrows to show heat being transferred from the flame to the bottom of the pot, from the bottom of the pot to the pot's sides, and from there to the pot's handle.

Conduction

Why do cooking pots often have plastic or rubberized handles?

_____

_____

_____

_____

ACTIVITY 18   Heat Radiation

Name:_____

Date:_____

When heat flows from the sun to Earth, much of it travels in a special kind of wave called infrared radiation. The sun produces infrared radiation. So do lightbulbs, campfires, and other heat sources. Dark-colored objects absorb (take in) infrared radiation. Light-colored objects reflect it, or bounce it back. Answer the questions about heat radiation.

1. Is it better to wear white or black outside on a hot summer day? Give a reason for your answer. _____

    _____

    _____

2. If you wanted to heat a bucket of water using only the sun, what color would you paint the bucket? Why? _____

    _____

    _____

ACTIVITY 19 Vacuums

Name:_____

Date:_____

A vacuum contains no matter. Even though there is no such thing as an absolute vacuum, outer space comes close. It contains very few molecules. When spacecraft need to get rid of extra heat, they must rely on radiation. Fans, which depend on convection, will not work in space. Use what you have learned about heat to answer the following questions on your own paper.

1. Why do fans depend on convection?

2. Why doesn't convection work in space?

3. A vacuum bottle keeps milk cold with a vacuum layer trapped between two layers of silvery glass. How does that vacuum keep heat away from the milk?

4. Pretend that you get to ask a scientific question about vacuums that could be answered by astronauts aboard a spacecraft. What would you ask? What evidence would be needed to answer your question?

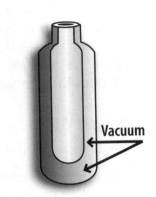

Vacuum

ACTIVITY 20 The History of Heat Measurement

Name:_____

Date:_____

In a thermometer, a column of heat-sensitive liquid, such as alcohol, expands inside a tube in a predictable way. A measurement scale is marked on the tube or on a backing plate. Circle the best answer. Use a dictionary if you need help.

1. This inventor of one of the world's first working telescopes also invented a water thermometer in 1593.
   - a. Benjamin Franklin
   - b. Galileo Galilei
   - c. Albert Einstein

2. In 1724, this German scientist invented the alcohol thermometer and the mercury thermometer and introduced the heat measurement scale still widely used in the United States.
   - a. Louis Pasteur
   - b. Galileo Galilei
   - c. Daniel Gabriel Fahrenheit

3. In 1742, this Swedish scientist developed a scale with 100 points, or degrees, between the freezing and boiling points of water.
   - a. Daniel Gabriel Fahrenheit
   - b. Anders Celsius
   - c. Lord William Thompson Kelvin

4. In 1848, this Scottish scientist developed a scale that begins at absolute zero. It is widely used by astronomers and other scientists.
   - a. Daniel Gabriel Fahrenheit
   - b. Anders Celsius
   - c. Lord William Thompson Kelvin

ACTIVITY 21 Conservation of Energy

Name:_____

Date:_____

Energy can never be created or destroyed. It merely changes form. This is called the Law of Conservation of Energy. Draw a diagram showing a floor lamp. In your picture, the lamp should be plugged into an electrical socket in the wall. An arrow should show energy flowing through the wire into the lamp. Wiggly arrows should show energy going out from the lamp into the room. Some of the arrows should be labeled "light." Others should be labeled "heat."

Challenge: Which type of lightbulb releases the most heat energy: fluorescent, incandescent, or LED? _____

Why does this make the bulb less efficient?

_____

_____

An Energy Chain

ACTIVITY 22 Conservation of Energy

Name:_____

Date:_____

An Energy Chain

Energy can never be created or destroyed. It merely changes form. This is called the Law of Conservation of Energy. Draw a diagram showing the sun shining on a tree. Draw an arrow from the sun to the tree. Label the arrow "energy." Under the tree, draw a fallen branch. Draw arrows to the tree's canopy of leaves and to the fallen branch. Label them "stored energy." Next, draw a campfire with two or three sticks and some flames. Draw arrows leading out from the flames. Label them "heat" and "light."

Challenge: Does this sheet of paper have any

energy?_____

Give a reason for your answer. _____

_____

ACTIVITY 23 Potential Energy & Kinetic Energy

Name:————————————

Date:————————————

There are two major types of energy: potential energy and kinetic energy. Potential energy is stored energy, or possible action. Kinetic energy is energy in motion, or energy in action. Read each example below and decide if each one has potential energy or kinetic energy. Circle the correct choice.

1. A roller coaster car at the top of a hill   potential energy   kinetic energy
2. A go-cart rolling down a hill   potential energy   kinetic energy
3. A pendulum at the top part of its swing   potential energy   kinetic energy
4. A large boulder resting on the side of a hill   potential energy   kinetic energy
5. Water behind a dam   potential energy   kinetic energy
6. An elevator going down   potential energy   kinetic energy

Challenge: If potential energy is stored energy, where does it come from? Choose one of the examples above and explain how the object obtained its potential energy. Don't forget the law of conservation of energy. ————————————————————
————————————————————————————————————

ACTIVITY 24 Kinetic Energy

Name:————————————

Date:————————————

The amount of kinetic energy an object contains depends on the object's mass and speed it is traveling. The more mass an object contains, and the faster it is going, the more kinetic energy it will have. For each problem, circle the choice that has the most kinetic energy.

1. a) a freight train going 60 mph
   b) a ball dropped from a balcony
   c) a bike coasting downhill
2. a) a clock pendulum at the top of its swing
   b) a satellite re-entering the atmosphere
   c) an Olympic skier racing down a slope
3. a) a pelican diving to catch a fish
   b) a gull circling on a thermal
   c) a boy fishing in a stream
4. a) an airplane landing
   b) a hummingbird landing on a branch
   c) a spacecraft landing in Florida
5. a) a meteorite as big as a house landing in the ocean
   b) a boy running downhill
   c) a rock as big as a fist falling into a well

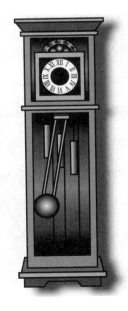

ACTIVITY 25   **Energy Roundup**

Name:_____

Date:_____

What do you remember about energy? Shade the circle of the best answer.

1. A hammer coming down on a nail is an example of

   (a.) conduction.   (b.) kinetic energy.   (c.) potential energy.

2. A car heater's fan works because of

   (a.) conduction.   (b.) convection.   (c.) the Fahrenheit scale.

3. Pots do not usually have metal handles because of

   (a.) conduction.   (b.) convection.   (c.) infrared radiation.

4. If water boils at 100 degrees at sea level you are using

   (a.) a broken thermometer.   (b.) the Celsius scale.   (c.) the Fahrenheit scale.

5. Heat

   (a.) flows.   (b.) disappears.   (c.) evaporates.

- -

ACTIVITY 26   **Energy Roundup**

Name:_____

Date:_____

What do you remember about energy? Read each statement and circle True or False.

1. Most substances contract, or fill less space, when they are heated.   True   False

2. Liquids turn into gases when they are cooled.   True   False

3. The most common gas in our atmosphere is oxygen.   True   False

4. Water is the only substance that turns into a solid when it is cooled.   True   False

5. Conduction can take place in solids.   True   False

6. A gas is a kind of fluid.   True   False

7. Observation is one kind of scientific evidence.   True   False

8. The three states of matter are solid, liquid, and energy.

   True   False

ACTIVITY 27 Mixtures

Name:_____

Date:_____

Mixtures contain two or more different substances. The substances in a mixture do not change. They can be separated. Mixtures can contain solids, liquids, and gases. Draw a line to connect the name of each mixture to the substances it contains.

1. seawater

2. soda pop

3. mustard

4. air

5. fruit salad

a. water, flavoring, carbon dioxide gas, sugar

b nitrogen, oxygen, carbon dioxide, and small amounts of other gases

c. water, sodium chloride, other dissolved minerals

d. apples, oranges, pineapple chunks, grapes, cherries

e. mustard seeds, vinegar, water, salt, turmeric

Challenge: Muddy water is a mixture. What would happen if you let a jar filled with muddy water sit undisturbed on a table for a few days? _____
_____

ACTIVITY 28 Suspensions

Name:_____

Date:_____

A suspension is one type of mixture. In a suspension, particles (pieces) of a solid float in a fluid (a liquid or gas). Draw a line to connect the name of each suspension to the substances it contains.

1. blood

2. paint

3. smoke

4. muddy water

5. fog

water, silt (fine dirt)

air, fine water droplets

plasma, red cells, white cells, platelets

air, ash, carbon monoxide, other gases

water, pigment (color), binder (glue)

Challenge: Write a scientific question about suspensions. Write one form of evidence a scientist could use to answer that question. _____
_____

ACTIVITY 29   Emulsions

Name:_____

Date:_____

     An emulsion is a special kind of mixture. Some liquids mix easily. For example, if you drop food coloring into water, it will mix, even if you do not stir it. Other liquids do not mix well. For example, if you pour some cooking oil into a glass of water, it will not mix. An emulsifier breaks up one of the liquids into droplets that can be suspended in the other liquid. Draw lines from each emulsion to its ingredients.

1. milk

2. salad dressing

3. peanut butter

4. mayonnaise

5. hand lotion

a. oil, wax, alcohol, water, and perfume

b. peanuts, peanut oil, salt, and sugar

c. water, lactose, fat, protein, minerals, and lecithin

d. oil, vinegar, water, salt and other spices, and honey

e. oil, vinegar, salt, egg yolks, and sugar

Challenge: If you make peanut butter in a food processor and you use only fresh peanuts, you will need to stir it each time you use it. Why? _____

_____

ACTIVITY 30   Solutions

Name:_____

Date:_____

     A solution is another kind of mixture. In a solution, a solute dissolves in a solvent. For example, if you put a spoonful of sugar into a cup of water, the sugar is the solute, and the water is the solvent. Use each clue to unscramble the word. Write it on the line.

1. In seawater, water is the solvent and salt is the O U E S T L _____.

2. If you pour sugar into water, water is the T O L S E N V _____.

3. Salt or sugar will S D I S V O L E _____ more quickly in warm water than in cold water.

4. Salt water is a O O N L U T S I _____.

5. Because salt can dissolve, it is O L U L S B E _____.

6. Because sand cannot dissolve, it is N S O B I L U L E

     _____.

Challenge: Write a scientific question about solutions. Write one kind of evidence a scientist might use to find the answer. _____

_____

ACTIVITY 31 Evaporation, Distillation, Filtration, Settling

Name:_____

Date:_____

There are several ways to separate the substances in a mixture. Read each clue and fill in the missing letters.

| evaporates | distillation | filter |
| centrifuging | settle | |

1. If you let a jar of muddy water sit on a shelf, the silt and sand will s __ __ __ l __. Then, you can pour the water off the top.
2. If you let a saltwater solution sit on a shelf, the water ev __ __ o __ __ t __ s, leaving salt crystals behind.
3. If you pour beach sand through a f __ __ t __ __, the sand will pass through, and shells will be trapped.
4. Sometimes, when water is heated, the steam is trapped. When the steam cools, it turns back into water. The water is very pure. Salts and other minerals are left behind. This process is called d __ __ t __ l __ a __ i __ n.
5. Suspensions are harder to separate. A machine spins the suspension around very fast. Solids cling to the sides of the container. The liquid is poured off. This is called c __ __ tr __ f __ __ __ __ __ g.

ACTIVITY 32 Mixture Roundup

Name:_____

Date:_____

What have you learned about mixtures? Answer each question.

1. Name three kinds of mixtures. _____, _____, and _____
2. Name four ways to separate substances in a mixture. _____, _____, _____, and _____
3. What does an emulsifier do? _____
4. Name four mixtures. _____, _____, _____, and _____

Challenge: If a suspension is a kind of mixture, and blood is a suspension, is blood a mixture? _____ On your own paper, draw a diagram to prove your answer.

ACTIVITY 33   Compounds

Name:_____

Date:_____

A compound is a combination of two or more elements. A compound is not a mixture. It is different from any of the elements it contains. For example, hydrogen and oxygen are elements. Each of them is a gas at room temperature. When hydrogen and oxygen combine, they become the compound water. Use the clues to unscramble the name of each compound.

1. I am a combination of sodium and chlorine. I taste great on chips.
    B E L A T   A S T L _____

2. I am a combination of carbon, hydrogen, and oxygen. I give lemons their tang.   I I C C T R   C I A D _____

3. I am a combination of hydrogen and oxygen. I can float a boat.
    A T W E R _____

4. I am a combination of silicon and oxygen. I am a very common mineral.
    Z U Q R T A _____

5. I am a combination of calcium, silicon, oxygen, and sodium. You can see right through me.
    S G A S L _____

- -

ACTIVITY 34   Organic Compounds

Name:_____

Date:_____

Compounds that contain carbon are special. They are sometimes called organic compounds because every living thing is made of carbon compounds. Read the clues, then fill in the missing words.

| seashells | aspirin | methane |
| dioxide | sugar | |

1. I am a combination of carbon, oxygen, and hydrogen. I am very sweet.
    I am _____.

2. I am a combination of carbon and hydrogen. I am used to heat homes.
    I am _____.

3. I am a combination of carbon and calcium called calcium carbonate. At the beach, you collect things made out of me. They are _____.

4. I am a combination of carbon and oxygen. I add fizz to soda. I am carbon
    _____.

5. I am a combination of carbon, hydrogen, and oxygen. I am a common medicine. I am
    _____.

ACTIVITY 35 Metals

Name:_____

Date:_____

Metals are everywhere. Discover what they have in common. Fill in the missing words.

> shiny   solid   electricity
>
> reacts   Metals   properties

1. _____ are special elements.

2. They all have certain _____ in common.

3. Pure metals are usually _____, not dull, when they are cut.

4. When the surface of a metal _____ with air or water, it can become dull or rough.

5. Metals conduct _____, which is why metals, such as copper, are used in wiring.

6. Mercury is the only metal that is not a _____ at room temperature.

ACTIVITY 36 Common Metals

Name:_____

Date:_____

Metals are shiny and they conduct electricity. All metals, except mercury, are solid at room temperature. Think about the metals you see every day. Circle either metal or not metal for each element.

1. oxygen   metal   not metal

2. gold   metal   not metal

3. iodine   metal   not metal

4. nickel   metal   not metal

5. silver   metal   not metal

ACTIVITY 37 Common Metals

Name:_____

Date:_____

Metals are shiny and they conduct electricity. All metals, except mercury, are solid at room temperature. Think about the metals you see every day. Write each item from the box in the correct column.

| aluminum | wood | tin | iron |
| plastic | helium | copper | glass |

Metal   **Not Metal**

_____   _____

_____   _____

_____   _____

_____   _____

ACTIVITY 38 Common Metals

Name:_____

Date:_____

We use metals in many ways. Draw a line to connect each metal to a common use.

1. iron   coatings for fancy forks, spoons, and knives

2. silver   frying pans and fence railings

3. copper   shields to protect people from X-rays

4. gold   pipes and electrical wiring

5. lead   wedding rings and crowns for teeth

Challenge: Name two more uses of metals. _____

_____

_____

_____

ACTIVITY 39 Alloys

Name:_____

Date:_____

A mixture of two or more metals is called an alloy.
Alloys combine the advantages of two or more metals. They are used in many ways. Use the clues to unscramble the name of each alloy.

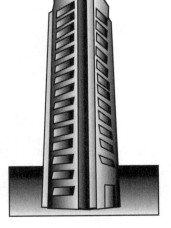

1. This alloy of copper and zinc is used to make trumpets and horns.

    R A S B A _____

2. This alloy of copper and tin is used to make sculptures.

    N Z B E R O _____

3. This silvery gray alloy of tin and lead is used to join wires together.

    S L E R D O _____

4. This alloy of iron and carbon is used in the frameworks of skyscrapers and bridges.

    T E L S E _____

5. This alloy of iron, carbon, and chromium is used to make spoons, forks, and knives.

    E S T A I N S L S   L E E T S _____

- -

ACTIVITY 40 Steel

Name:_____

Date:_____

Steel is everywhere. Find out more about it.
Use the clues to unscramble each word.

1. Steel is an L O A L Y _____.

2. It is mostly R I N O _____.

3. It contains a small, but important, amount of A C O N R B

    _____.

4. Steel is a E L T A M _____, so it conducts

    electricity.

5. Because it contains R I N O _____, steel at-

    tracts A G T S N E M _____.

Challenge: List three things made of steel in your classroom or at home. _____

ACTIVITY 41 Nonmetals

Name:_____

Date:_____

About three-fourths of all elements are metals.
The rest are nonmetals. They are not shiny when cut and they are not good conductors of electricity. Use the word box to fill in the blanks.

> nitrogen   carbon   sulfur   hydrogen
> selenium   oxygen   phosphorus

1. Three nonmetals found in the atmosphere are:

    _____, _____, and _____.

2. All forms of life on Earth have _____ in their tissues.

3. Used in medicines and in matches, _____ smells like rotten eggs.

4. Fertilizers and toothpaste are just two of the products that use_____.

5. In addition to being in colored glass, _____ is also used in fertilizers

    and animal feeds.

ACTIVITY 42 Nonmetals

Name:_____

Date:_____

Noble gases, semimetals, and halogens are types
of nonmetals. Find out more about them. Use the word box to fill in the blanks.

> chlorine   elements   electricity   gases
> metals   helium   solar

Noble _____ do not combine with other

elements. Neon and _____ are familiar noble

gases. Semimetals are like _____ in some ways and like nonmetals in

other ways. Silicon, which conducts _____ under certain conditions,

is a semimetal. It is used in _____ panels and electronic equipment.

Halogens combine easily with other _____ to form salts. For example,

_____, a halogen, combines with sodium to form table salt.

ACTIVITY 43 Nonmetals

Name:_____

Date:_____

About three-fourths of all elements are metals.
The rest are nonmetals. Label the chart using the word box.

1. _____

4. _____

5. _____

6. _____

2. _____

3. _____

```
elements        metals
nonmetals       noble gases
semimetals      halogens
```

ACTIVITY 44 Crystals

Name:_____

Date:_____

Have you ever grown salt crystals? If you have,
you know that they take the form of little cubes. Fill in the missing letters to find out more about crystals.

1. A crystal is a special type of s __ __ __ d.

2. The m __ l __ c __ __ __ s inside a crystal are lined up in a certain way.

3. The way the molecules line up depends on their st __ __ __ t __ r __ .

4. The shapes of crystals help geologists identify m __ n __ __ __ l __ .

5. Crystals have flat s __ __ __ a __ __ s called faces.

6. Each of these __ __ __ __ s has a shape.

7. Some crystal faces are tr __ __ n __ __ l __ r.

8. Others are square or __ __ x __ g __ __ a __ .

Challenge: Dissolve salt in a cup filled with warm water. Put a piece of cotton string in the cup so one end hangs over the cup's rim and the other end sits in the water. Place the cup in a place where it will not be disturbed. Come back in a week or more. What do you see?

ACTIVITY 45   Crystals

Name:_____

Date:_____

Crystals come in many shapes and sizes. Some of them are very hard. Others are so delicate that they can melt away. Draw lines to match each substance with its description.

1. a clear cube formed from sodium chloride   snow

2. a very hard, valuable gem, often clear   glass

3. plate-like six-sided water crystals formed in clouds   quartz

4. a crystal containing silica; common in sand   table salt

5. a transparent solid that is not a crystal   diamond

ACTIVITY 46   Chemical Reactions

Name:_____

Date:_____

Chemical reactions can be exciting. Find out more about them by filling in the missing letters.

1. A ch __ __ i __ __ l reaction changes substances into different substances.

2. The original substances can be elements or c __ __ p __ __ n __ s.

3. Because they react with one another, the original substances are called re __ __ t __ n __ s.

4. After the substances interact, they are called pr __ du __ __ s.

5. You can see a chemical reaction if you place a penny on a vinegar-soaked p __ __ __ r towel.

6. The p __ __ __ y turns green.

7. The co __ __ er in the penny reacts with oxygen to form copper oxide.

8. Copper oxide is completely different from both copper and o __ __ g __ n.

ACTIVITY 47 Chemical Reactions

Name:_____

Date:_____

Chemical reactions are different from physical reactions. After a chemical reaction, the product or products are different from the original re-actants. Remember: physical reactions can change states, sizes, shapes, or mixtures, but the elements in a mixture are not changed into compounds. Write each change from the box in the correct column.

| a can rusting | a can being crushed | paper being cut |
| natural gas burning | a penny turning green | sugar dissolving in water |

Chemical Changes   **Physical Changes**

_____   _____

_____   _____

_____   _____

Challenge: Name another chemical change and another physical change. _____

_____

ACTIVITY 48 Acids

Name:_____

Date:_____

There are three special kinds of compounds. They are acids, bases, and neutral substances. You can find acids and bases in your home. Use the clues to unscramble the names of these common acids.

1. I am found in lemons.   R I C C I T _____ acid

2. I am found in vinegar.   C E T A I C _____ acid

3. I help to tan leather.   A T N I C N _____ acid

4. I put the fizz in soda.   R B O C C N I A _____ acid

5. I am Vitamin C.   I C S C A B O R _____ acid

Challenge: Some household acids are dangerous. Name one of them. _____

ACTIVITY 49   Bases

Name:_____

Date:_____

Bases that dissolve in water are called alkalis.
Circle the name of the base that matches each clue.

1.	A good source of calcium	soap	milk	toothpaste
2.	Often found in window cleaner	milk	detergent	ammonia
3.	Great for dental care	soap	apricots	toothpaste
4.	Makes the refrigerator smell fresh	milk	baking soda	raisins
5.	Kills germs on your hands	baking soda	soap	milk

Challenge: Some household products containing alkalis are very dangerous.

Name one of them. _____

ACTIVITY 50   Acids and Bases:
The Litmus Test

Name:_____

Date:_____

Testing solutions to find out whether they are acids, bases, or neutral is fun. The easiest way to test liquids is to use litmus paper. This special paper comes in red or blue strips. Testing requires both. Acids turn blue litmus paper red. Bases turn red litmus paper blue. In neutral solutions, both colors of litmus paper stay the same. Circle the right choice for each liquid.

1.	lemon juice	blue to red	no change	red to blue
2.	toothpaste	blue to red	no change	red to blue
3.	soap	blue to red	no change	red to blue
4.	vinegar	blue to red	no change	red to blue
5.	vitamin C solution	blue to red	no change	red to blue
6.	distilled water	blue to red	no change	red to blue

Challenge: Explain why you can't test for acids and bases with only one color of litmus paper.

ACTIVITY 51   Acids and Bases

Name:_____

Date:_____

When acids meet bases, a special chemical reaction takes place. We say that bases and acids neutralize each other. It is always a good idea to mix acids and bases only with the help of an experienced adult. Use the word box to complete the paragraph.

| alkali | atmosphere | dioxide | reaction |
| chemical | neutralize | baking soda | Vinegar |

_____ is mildly acid. Baking soda is mildly _____.

When vinegar and _____ mix, they _____

each other. This chemical reaction has been used for many science fair projects. When red

food coloring is added to the baking soda, the _____ creates an impres-

sive erupting volcano. How does it work? When you add vinegar to baking soda and water, the

_____ reaction creates the gas carbon _____. It

bubbles up as it moves out into the _____.

ACTIVITY 52   Sorting It All Out

Name:_____

Date:_____

Substances can be sorted in different ways. In which groups do these common items belong? Circle all of the terms that fit each item.

1. vinegar in water

    acid   base   fluid   emulsion   liquid

2. soap in water

    acid   base   fluid   mixture   liquid

3. carbon dioxide

    product   fluid   gas   organic compound

4. water

    acid   base   fluid   suspension   solution   mixture   compound

5. brass

    solid   fluid   metal   nonmetal   alloy   conductor   magnetic

ACTIVITY 53   The Carbon Cycle

Name:_____

Date:_____

Carbon dioxide and oxygen make life on Earth possible. Study the diagram. Fill in the blanks with the words from the box.

> material   burn   decay
> energy   carbon dioxide

1. Photosynthesis in the leaves of green plants changes _____ and sunlight into sugar and oxygen.

2. When plants _____ in a fire, carbon dioxide is released.

3. The cells of living animals create carbon dioxide when they use _____.

4. After plants and animals die, their bodies _____.

5. Decaying plant and animal _____ releases carbon dioxide.

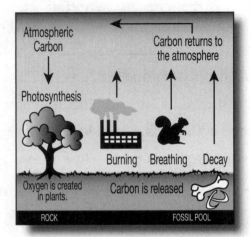

ACTIVITY 54   Carbon Cycle: Energy in Storage

Name:_____

Date:_____

Scientists believe that much of the energy we use to fuel our cars and run our factories was created by the carbon cycle long ago. Use the word box to fill in the blanks.

> layers   Coal   forests   fossil fuels   sea
> rock   Petroleum   oil   animals   cycle

Long ago tiny _____ and plants lived in the _____.

After they died and sank to the sea floor, they were buried by _____

of silt and sand. Those layers of sediment eventually turned to _____.

The bodies of the little creatures turned into _____.

_____ is really carbon _____ energy,

stored for many years. _____ is also stored energy. It

comes from ancient _____ and swamps. Coal and

oil are called _____.

ACTIVITY 55   Natural Fibers

Name:_____

Date:_____

We use fibers to make rope, clothing, and other products. Natural fibers come from plants and animals. Match the following natural fibers to the materials from which they are made.

1. silk

2. wool

3. cotton

4. linen

5. yarn

6. loom

spun fibers that can be knit or woven into cloth

equipment used to weave cloth

cloth made from the cocoons of certain caterpillars

cloth made from the fuzzy head of a plant

cloth made from the fleece of sheep

cloth made from stems of the flax plant

Challenge: Name something made from natural fibers. _____

_____

ACTIVITY 56   Synthetic Fibers

Name:_____

Date:_____

Synthetic fibers are man-made. Find out more about them. Use the word box to fill in the blanks.

polyester	acrylic	rayon	nylon
pulp	chemicals	synthetic	plant

Fabric Content:
Polyester 85%
Rayon   10%
Nylon   5%

Many of us wear clothes made out of _____ fibers.

These clothes are easy to care for. They do not wrinkle easily, and they last a long time.

Some synthetic fibers, such as _____, start out with wood

_____, coconut husks, or other _____

materials. The plant materials are treated with _____

and then spun into yarns. Other fibers such as _____,

_____, and _____ are made from petroleum.

Challenge: Name something made from synthetic fibers. _____

_____

ACTIVITY 57 **Chemical Changes Roundup**

Name:_____

Date:_____

What do you remember about chemical changes? Shade the circle of the best choice.

1. A synthetic fabric is
   - (a.) man-made.
   - (b.) a fossil fuel.
   - (c.) part of the carbon cycle.

2. The following is created during the carbon cycle:
   - (a.) alkali.
   - (b.) carbon dioxide.
   - (c.) synthetic fiber.

3. The formation of copper oxide is
   - (a.) a chemical reaction.
   - (b.) part of a litmus test.
   - (c.) part of the carbon cycle.

4. When an acid meets a base,
   - (a.) nothing happens.
   - (b.) the acid gets stronger.
   - (c.) the acid neutralizes the base.

5. Litmus paper is used to test for
   - (a.) acids.
   - (b.) poisonous gases.
   - (c.) oxygen.

ACTIVITY 58 **Chemical Changes Roundup**

Name:_____

Date:_____

What do you remember about chemical changes? Match the word to the correct description.

_____ 1. coal

_____ 2. polyester

_____ 3. lemon juice

_____ 4. alkali

_____ 5. carbon dioxide

_____ 6. baking soda and vinegar

_____ 7. iron oxide

a. create an acid/base reaction

b. part of the carbon cycle

c. any base soluble in water

d. turns blue litmus paper red

e. a fossil fuel

f. rust

g. made from petroleum

ACTIVITY 59 Gravity

Name:_____

Date:_____

What's so important about gravity? Find out.
Unscramble the words and write them on the lines to complete each sentence.

1. Gravity is a R O E C F _____.

2. It A A T S C T T R _____, or pulls, everything.

3. Suns, moons, and planets have R A Y V I T G _____.

4. Even a E N C P I L _____ or a playground ball has gravity.

5. Every E C O T B J _____ attracts every other object with its gravity.

6. Objects with greater A S M A _____, such as Earth, have more
   V I T A T I N A L G R A O _____ attraction than objects
   with less mass, such as a person, or even a skyscraper.

Challenge: Write a scientific question about gravity. Include one type of scientific evidence you
might use to answer it. _____

_____

ACTIVITY 60 Magnetism and Gravity

Name:_____

Date:_____

Find out how these two important forces are the same
and how they are different. Shade in the bubble for the best choice.

1. Both magnetism and gravity are

   (a.) chemical changes.   (b.) visible.   (c.) forces.

2. Both magnetism and gravity are forces of

   (a.) attraction.   (b.) chemical change. (c.) decay.

3. Every object pulls on every other object with

   (a.) string.   (b.) magnetism.   (c.) gravity.

4. Magnetism attracts

   (a.) every object.   (b.) only objects that are magnetic. (c.) only copper pennies.

5. The earth does not have its own

   (a.) magnetic field.   (b.) invisibility shield.   (c.) gravity.

ACTIVITY 61   Magnetism

Name:_____

Date:_____

What do you know about magnets and magnetism?
Fill in the missing letters to complete each sentence.

1. Every magnet has two p __ l __ s.

2. They have opposite c __ __ r __ es.

3. One is north and the other is s __ __ __ h.

4. If you have two magnets, the north and south poles will p __ __ __ on each other.

5. If you have two magnets, the south and south poles will __ __ sh each other away.

6. To __ __ __ el means to push away.

7. To __ __ __ r __ __ t means to pull toward.

ACTIVITY 62   Magnetic Fields

Name:_____

Date:_____

The influence of a magnet extends beyond its poles.
The area that a magnet influences with its attraction is called a magnetic field. Label each diagram.

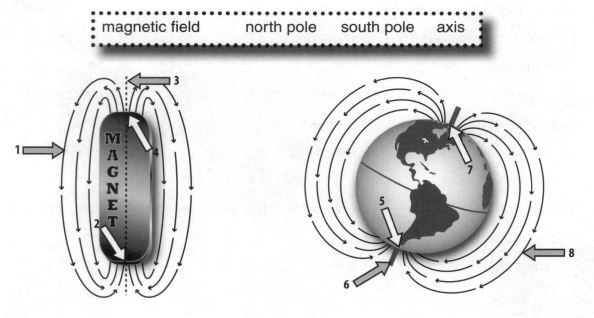

magnetic field   north pole   south pole   axis

ACTIVITY 63   Electricity

Name: _____

Date: _____

Humankind's interest in electricity dates back more than 2,500 years. Read the paragraph and answer the questions.

The word *electricity* comes from the Greek word *elektron*. It means amber. Amber is fossilized tree sap. It picks up an electrical charge easily. The Greeks made a discovery. They found out that they could rub a piece of amber on a piece of fur and then use it to pick up light objects, such as feathers.

1. What is amber? _____

2. What does the Greek word *elektron* mean? _____

3. Name an easy way to add a charge to a piece of amber. _____

   _____

4. What can you pick up with a piece of charged amber? _____

   _____

5. Did the ancient Greeks have lightbulbs? _____

ACTIVITY 64   Electrostatics: The Branch of Science Behind the Zap

Name: _____

Date: _____

Have you ever made pieces of paper dance with a comb? Complete the exercise to find out more about this electrifying phenomenon. Use the clues to help underline the hidden word in each group of letters.

1. The study of electrical charges is called M E T I C E L E C T R O S T A T I C S R C K B D S.

2. When you rub a balloon on a wall, the balloon becomes
   B C R E C H A R G E D S D F H K D F C H S A P.

3. Charged objects T C A S T A T T R A C T T S D C K R E objects that are not charged.

4. All matter is made up of tiny T T O A T O M S Y T C O M M T O S.

5. Atoms are made up of protons and L E C T S R I D E L E C T R O N S B R E W C X L C N S.

6. Pro often means "for," which will help you remember that protons have a
   N E B G I T P O S I T I V E R T Y P O L D F H charge.

7. Electrons have the opposite charge, which is U N H P O S J N E G A T I V E P O M I V G K.

8. On a dry winter day, comb your hair. The comb takes some electrons from your hair. Since the comb has borrowed some of your hair's electrons, it now has more electrons than protons. That gives the comb a P O S R T V B N E G A T I V E S I T T P O S charge.

9. The comb will R R T T I U B A T T R A C T P C C E A R E O E L little pieces of paper.

ACTIVITY 65 Lightning

Name: _____

Date: _____

Lightning is a dramatic form of electricity.
Use the word box to fill in the blanks.

balancing	electrons	Positively	base
bolt	thunderstorm	ions	charged

During a _____, some atoms gain electrons. They become

negatively _____. Atoms that have gained or lost an electron are

called _____. _____ charged ions move toward

the top of the cloud. Negatively charged ions stay near the _____

of a cloud. Many objects on the ground are positively charged. The negatively charged

ions at the base of the cloud have extra _____ and need

to discharge them. Like the spark that travels from your hand to a doorknob, a

_____ of lightning is a _____ of electrons.

Challenge: Why is it dangerous to be outdoors just before or during a lightning storm?

_____

ACTIVITY 66 Benjamin Franklin and His Famous Kite

Name: _____

Date: _____

Benjamin Franklin was gifted in many fields. Find out
more about him by shading in the circle of the best choice.

Franklin

1. Benjamin Franklin was not
   - (a.) a Founding Father.
   - (b.) a singer.
   - (c.) an inventor and scientist.
2. Benjamin Franklin experimented with
   - (a.) telephones.
   - (b.) satellites.
   - (c.) electricity.
3. Benjamin Franklin sent up a kite
   - (a.) before a thunderstorm.
   - (b.) during a thunderstorm.
   - (c.) after a thunderstorm.
4. Benjamin Franklin wanted to
   - (a.) light his bedroom.
   - (b.) make an electrical key.
   - (c.) collect electricity.
5. A Russian scientist who tried to repeat the experiment during a thunderstorm was
   - (a.) more famous.
   - (b.) killed.
   - (c.) successful.

ACTIVITY 67　Flowing Current

Name:_____

Date:_____

Electricity is all around us. It helps us with many tasks every day. Find out more about the way it moves. Use the word box to fill in the blanks and complete the paragraph.

```
plastic      insulator      current      Electrons
flow         atom           metal        electricity
```

_____ can move along a wire. This is how _____ reaches us to light our homes and run our appliances. It is called electric _____ because it seems to _____ like water in a stream. Wires are made of materials that are good conductors. Most wires are _____. Inside the wire, electrons skip from one _____ to the next. Electrical wires are usually coated with _____. The atoms in plastic do not give up their electrons easily, so electricity cannot flow through it. A substance that keeps electricity from passing through it is an _____.

ACTIVITY 68　Galvanometer

Name:_____

Date:_____

Many of the units we use for measuring different aspects of electricity are named after scientists and scholars who were pioneers in the field. In the early 1800s, Leopold Nobili invented an instrument to measure the flow of electricity through a wire. He named his device a galvanometer after Luigi Galvani, an 18th century researcher. Later, James Joule used a galvanometer in his experiments with resistance and heat. A modern unit of energy, the joule, is named after him.

Galvani

1. What did a galvanometer measure? _____
   _____

2. Who invented the galvanometer? _____

3. How did James Joule use the galvanometer? _____
   _____

4. What is named after James Joule? _____

Challenge: If you invented something, what would you name it? Why? _____
_____

ACTIVITY 69 Electricity From Chemicals

Name:_____

Date:_____

Electricity does not always flow through wires to reach us. Sometimes, it is created by chemical reactions. We use batteries in flashlights, cell phones, and automobiles. The electricity that comes from batteries is produced as the result of chemical reactions. A battery contains an anode, which produces negative ions, and a cathode, or positive electrode, that absorbs, or soaks up, the extra electrons and completes the circuit. Inside a dry cell battery, a rod of carbon is the cathode. The anode is a small cup of zinc. Lead and acid batteries are used in cars. Nickel and cadmium react in rechargeable batteries.

1. Is electricity stored inside a battery? _____
2. What does an anode produce? _____
3. What does a cathode do? _____
4. Which elements are used in rechargeable batteries? _____
5. What are some uses of batteries? _____
    _____

ACTIVITY 70 Conductors and Insulators

Name:_____

Date:_____

Electric currents flow easily through substances with many loosely held electrons. These are called conductors. Currents do not flow through substances with no free electrons. Plastic, ceramic, and glass are insulators. Match the terms to their definitions.

____ 1. conductor
____ 2. insulator
____ 3. metals
____ 4. glass
____ 5. water

a. a good conductor that is not a solid or a metal
b. an insulator that you can see through
c. a substance that allows electrons to move easily
d. elements often used to make wires
e. a substance that does not allow electrons to move freely

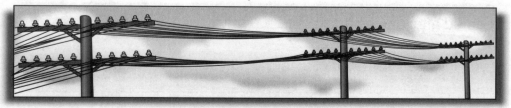

ACTIVITY 71 Circuits

Name: _____

Date: _____

Electricity flows from areas where there are too many electrons to areas where there are not enough. The path of this flow is called a circuit. If the circuit is broken, electricity will stop flowing. That is how switches work. A switch breaks the circuit, and the flow of electricity stops. When a piece of conductive material slides over the break, the current flows again. Label each part of the diagram.

electrons   flow   positive

switch   light   battery

negative

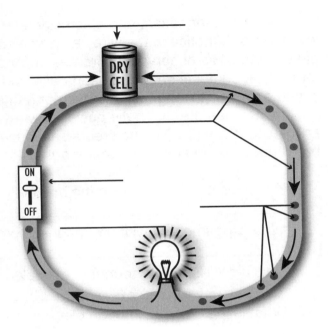

ACTIVITY 72 Resistance

Name: _____

Date: _____

If you are standing in a doorway, and someone tries to push by you but you do not let them pass, you are resisting that person. Find out about electrical resistance when you unscramble these words.

1. In some wires, electrons jump from atom to atom easily. In others, they travel slowly, pushing their way through the atoms in the metal. This is called T A S C E N R E S I _____.

2. Resistance causes a build-up of E T H A _____.

3. Some electric appliances use the heat caused by resistance. This is how E R S A S T T O _____, O N I R S _____, and H E R E A T S _____ work.

4. Inside an incandescent lightbulb, resistance in a fine tungsten wire called a A M E N T F I L _____ creates light.

5. Georg Ohm studied resistance. The standard unit of resistance M E M A E N T S U R E _____, the ohm, is named after him.

ACTIVITY 73 Magnetism and Electricity

Name:_____

Date:_____

Ampere

How are magnetism and electricity related? Hans Christian Oersted was the first to notice that a wire carrying electric current attracted a compass needle. His observations interested Andre Marie Ampere, who performed experiments showing that parallel wires carrying current behaved, in some ways, like magnets. An inventor named William Sturgeon learned how to increase the magnetic power of wires. He wrapped a wire around an insulated iron rod. He had created an electromagnet. An electromagnet has a huge advantage over other magnets. It can be turned on and off.

1. Who was the first to notice the magnetic properties of electric current?
   _____

2. Who experimented with the magnetic properties of electric current in parallel wires?
   _____

3. How did William Sturgeon make an electromagnet?
   _____

4. What is the advantage of an electromagnet?
   _____

ACTIVITY 74 Magnetism and Electricity

Name:_____

Date:_____

Complete the activity to discover some of the uses of electromagnets. Unscramble each word and fill in the blank.

1. Huge electromagnets lift A I L E S M U T O B O _____ in scrap yards.

2. Electromagnets quickly sort steel cans from L U U A M I N M
   _____ cans at recycling centers.

3. After an accident, precision electromagnets can remove metal I A R T C L E P S
   _____ from an eye.

4. Special electromagnets, along with radio waves, help doctors look into their patients' bodies with M G T I C N E A
   _____ Resonance Imaging.

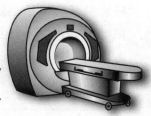

5. A train developed in Germany hovers above the rail, powered by R O M E L E C T E T A G N S _____.

ACTIVITY 75 Michael Faraday

Name:_____

Date:_____

One of the most important uses of electromagnetism is in electric motors. Find out more about one of the men who made them possible, Michael Faraday, by filling in the blanks.

> electromagnetism   motion   electricity   scientists   Generators

1. Michael Faraday worked with other _____ in the 1820s and 1830s.

2. They were looking for a way to turn electricity into _____.

3. They knew that _____ was the key.

4. Faraday discovered ways to use magnetic fields to control the flow of _____.

5. _____, transformers, and electric motors would not have been possible without his work.

Faraday

ACTIVITY 76 Tesla and the AC Motor

Name:_____

Date:_____

Find out about the man who invented alternating current by reading the paragraph and answering the questions.

A scientist named Nikola Tesla made many important discoveries about electricity. He studied the ideas of Faraday and others. In 1888, he built an induction motor. Tesla's motor ran on alternating current, or AC. It contained two sets of wires coiled around a central shaft. The shaft was called a rotor. Electrical currents that changed direction quickly caused the rotor to turn.

1. What did Nikola Tesla study? _____

2. When did Tesla build his motor? _____

3. What part of the motor turned? _____

4. What does *alternating* mean? _____

5. In what way does AC power alternate? _____

Tesla

ACTIVITY 77) Home Uses of Electricity

Name:_____

Date:_____

Electricity is part of our lives. In each list, circle the things that do not need electricity to operate. Be careful! Batteries generate electricity.

1. television   radio   oil lamp   mixer
2. bicycle   traffic signal desk light   computer
3. digital watch   printer   car   garden hose
4. refrigerator   dishwasher   binoculars   stereo
5. cell phone   charcoal grill blender   washing machine

Challenge: Blackouts happen. What would you miss the most if the electricity in your home were off for a day or a week? What could you do to prepare for a temporary loss of electric service? _____

_____

ACTIVITY 78) Communicating With Electricity

Name:_____

Date:_____

Shade the circle of the best choice.

| Bell |

1. One of the first uses of electricity was
    (a.) the refrigerator.   (b.) the computer.   (c.) the telegraph.
2. To send a telegraph message, pulses of electric current were sent through
    (a.) wires using Morse code. (b.) voice mail.   (c.) fax images.
3. In the 1870s, Alexander Graham Bell developed a device to send sound through wires. It was a
    (a.) telegraph.   (b.) telephone.   (c.) radio.
4. In 1901, Guglielmo Marconi sent a message from England to Newfoundland without wires. The message was sent by
    (a.) satellite.   (b.) telephone.   (c.) radio.
5. In the 1920s, Vladimir Zworykin developed ways to change pictures into electrical signals that could be sent out, or broadcast. His work led to the development of
    (a.) television.   (b.) radio.   (c.) satellites.

ACTIVITY 79 Electricity Roundup

Name: _____

Date: _____

Find out what you remember about electricity by matching.

_____ 1. electricity

_____ 2. a conductor

_____ 3. anode

_____ 4. ion

_____ 5. zinc

_____ 6. an insulator

a. an element used in batteries

b. a charged atom

c. plastic

d. copper

e. substance that produces negative ions

f. electrons flowing from areas of high concentration to areas of low concentration

ACTIVITY 80 Electricity Roundup

Name: _____

Date: _____

What do you remember about great scientists?
Draw a line to match each clue to the name of a great scientist or thinker.

1. resistance

2. magnetic properties of electricity

3. alternating current

4. control the flow of electricity

5. collection of electricity from lightning

Faraday

Franklin

Ohm

Tesla

Ampere

Tesla

Ampere

ACTIVITY 81 Work

Name:_____

Date:_____

Work is a force that causes displacement. For example, if you lift a book off a table, work has been performed. Energy has been transferred from you to the book. Finish the chart.

1.

player $\xrightarrow[\text{energy}]{\text{work}}$ bat $\longrightarrow$ ball

2.

_____ _____ _____ _____ pins

3.

_____ _____ _____ _____ nail

ACTIVITY 82 Wedges

Name:_____

Date:_____

A wedge is a simple machine. It uses a pair of inclined planes to make a small force more powerful. An ax is a good example of a wedge. Circle the wedge in each group.

1. car tire   ax   seesaw
2. front tooth bike wheel elevator
3. scooter   snowplow   wheelbarrow
4. doorknob   rubber band chisel
5. hammer   nail   box
6. backrest   mattress   night stand

Challenge: Draw or name another device that includes a wedge. _____

_____

ACTIVITY 83 **Ramps**

Name: _____

Date: _____

An inclined plane, or ramp, is a slope. It increases distance and makes it easier to raise a heavy object from one point to another. Unscramble the name of each inclined plane.

1. eelcairwhh rmpa   _____

2. aeewfry omnrap   _____

3. idbgre cproapah   _____

4. ovmgin avn oalindg rpam   _____

5. hisp's gpnglanak   _____

ACTIVITY 84 **The Wheel**

Name: _____

Date: _____

The wheel makes work easier in many ways. Fill in the missing letters to create a list of devices that include a wheel.

1. F __ __ r __ s wh __ __ l   _____

2. w __ __ __ rw __ __ el   _____

3. st __ __ __ i __ g w __ __ el   _____

4. f __ n   _____

5. s __ in __ __ ng w __ __ __ l   _____

Challenge: List another example of a useful wheel. _____

_____

ACTIVITY 85 Wheels and Axles

Name: _____

Date: _____

Wheels and axles are found on trains, cars, and trucks. This simple machine is also part of countless complex machines. Circle the item that contains a wheel and axle in each set.

1. freeway onramp   doorknob   ax

2. zipper   seesaw   skateboard

3. bike   front tooth   arm

4. backpack with pockets   briefcase with lock   rolling suitcase

Challenge: Draw a wheel and axle.

ACTIVITY 86 Screws

Name: _____

Date: _____

A screw is a useful simple machine. If you look at a screw carefully, you will see that it is really a ramp spiraling around a central core. The spiral makes the ramp longer, and that makes each part of the work easier. Find an example of a screw in each line. Circle it, and then write it on the line.

1. bulscrspiralstaircasebodrjoin _____ _____

2. jatyespboltthrpiconnhosew _____

3. spibocorkscrewjoiyhtrctihs _____

4. corscrspijarlidthreadralst _____ _____ _____

5. jatpldhsedrillbitvsebomett _____ _____

6. bltmmxcflightbulbendrep _____ _____

ACTIVITY 87   Levers

Name: _____

Date: _____

Levers are powerful simple machines. A seesaw is a good example. Force or effort is applied to one side of the lever to lift a load or overcome some resistance on the other side. The balance point of a lever is called the fulcrum. In a seesaw, the fulcrum is in the middle.

Directions: Circle the items that are NOT levers. Write the levers on the lines.

seesawaxonrampbicyclewheelbicyclehandbrakeswheelbarrowbottleopenertoilethandle gardenhoseendnailclipperstaplerscrewnailarmnoseeartongstweezerscandle

1. _____   2. _____

3. _____   4. _____

5. _____   6. _____

7. _____   8. _____

9. _____   10. _____

ACTIVITY 88   Fulcrums

Name: _____

Date: _____

A fulcrum is the balance point of a lever. Sometimes, it is a triangular piece of metal or wood. Other times, it is an invisible point. For example, when you press down on one end of a shovel to lift a rock, you are using a lever, but the balance point, or fulcrum, cannot be seen.

1. Draw a picture of a seesaw. Label the load and the fulcrum. Draw an arrow to show where effort is being applied. Label the arrow force.
2. Draw a picture of a shovel lifting the edge of a rock out of the ground. Draw an arrow to show where the force is being applied. Label the load.

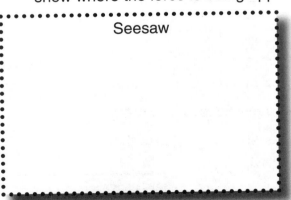

Seesaw

Shovel

ACTIVITY 89 Pivots

Name:_____

Date:_____

The word *pivot* describes a kind of action. When something pivots, it turns. Use the word box to complete each sentence.

> bolt   wrench   turning point   hinge   fulcrum

1. A pivot is a _____.

2. The bar or plank of a lever pivots on its _____.

3. You can use a _____,

   which is a lever, to loosen a bolt.

4. When you are loosening the bolt, the pivot is the

   _____.

5. When you open a door, the pivot is the

   _____.

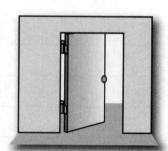

ACTIVITY 90 Pulleys

Name:_____

Date:_____

Pulleys are another simple machine. They use at least one wheel and some rope or chain to make certain kinds of work easier. Use the word box to complete the paragraph.

> distance   load   crane
>
> machine   pull   pulley
>
> energy   raise   force

Have you ever watched someone _____ or lower

a flag on a pole? If so, you have seen a _____ in action.

A pulley makes it easier to lift a _____. Like the screw, it

lowers the amount of effort or _____ needed by increas-

ing _____. For example, you probably noticed how many

times the person had to _____ on the rope to raise that

flag. He was applying _____ to a simple _____.

A construction _____ is a large and impressive example of a pulley.

ACTIVITY 91) Complex Machines

Name: _____

Date: _____

There are just six simple machines. They are the inclined plane or ramp, the wedge, the screw, the wheel and axle, the lever, and the pulley. The six simple machines combine in many ways to make cars, factory equipment, appliances, and hundreds of other complex machines we use every day. Write the name of each machine in the correct column.

| rolling pin | automobile | switchback on a trail |
| bicycle | spiral staircase | backhoe |

Simple Machine   **Complex Machine**

_____   _____

_____   _____

_____   _____

ACTIVITY 92) Gears

Name: _____

Date: _____

Unscramble the words and write them on the lines to complete the paragraph.

Gears are two or more E D O O T T H _____ wheels. They E M S H _____, or interlock, with each other. Each gear turns the one E S B I D E _____ it. In this way, gears I A N S T T R M _____, or send, energy from one place to another. Each gear in a series turns in the P O S O I T P E _____ direction from the one next to it. Smaller gears turn more I C K Q L U Y _____ than larger gears, but larger gears are S I R E E A _____ to turn. This will not be a surprise if you remember that longer I S T A E N C D _____ helped ramps, screws, and pulleys to work with less F O E F R T _____ at any one time. Gears are used in many complex machines. You may have seen them in C K S C L O _____ and bicycles.

Challenge: When you are going up a hill on a 10 speed bicycle, will your chain settle on (engage) a large gear or a small one? Why? _____

_____

ACTIVITY 93 Simple Machines Roundup

Name:_____

Date:_____

What do you know about simple machines? Match each type of simple machine to an example.

_____ 1. screw   a. ax

_____ 2. wheel and axle   b. spiral staircase

_____ 3. lever   c. switchback on a hiking trail

_____ 4. pulley   d. doorknob

_____ 5. inclined plane   e. seesaw

_____ 6. wedge   f. flag pole end

Challenge: Name two more examples of simple machines. Explain why each one is useful.

_____

_____

ACTIVITY 94 Work and Machines Roundup

Name:_____

Date:_____

What have you learned about work and machines? Put it all together with this quick review. Use the clues to fill in the blanks.

| inclined plane | fulcrum | work |
| complex machine | machine | |

1. The transfer of force, energy, or effort to an object
   _____

2. Any device that increases force or distance to make work easier
   _____

3. A device that combines two or more simple machines _____

4. The balance point or pivot of a lever _____

5. a slope _____

Challenge: Are you doing work when you hit a wooden backstop with a ball? Give a reason for your answer. _____

_____

ACTIVITY 95 Galileo's Motion Experiments

Name: _____

Date: _____

Use the words in the box to complete the paragraph about one of the most famous motion experiments of all time.

exactly	vacuum	bottom	released
same	object	hammer	faster

Imagine that a ten-pound weight and a one-pound weight are hung at the top of a _____ chamber. Both weights are _____ at exactly the same time. Which one will reach the _____ of the chamber first? It seems to make sense that the heavier weight will fall much _____, but it is not true.

Galileo

Galileo Galilei discovered that the mass of an _____ does not determine how fast it will fall. He proved that both a heavy weight and a light weight will land at _____ the same time. During the Apollo 15 mission to the moon in 1971, astronaut David Scott dropped a _____ and a feather. Both landed on the lunar surface at the _____ time!

ACTIVITY 96 Sir Isaac Newton: Gravity and Motion

Name: _____

Date: _____

Although Isaac Newton probably was not struck on the head by a falling apple, he is famous for his observations about gravity. Scientists also remember him for his observations about force and motion. Find out more about this world-changing thinker. Unscramble each word and write it on the line.

SIR ISAAC NEWTON

Sir Isaac (tNnewo) _____ was a great British scientist. About 300 years ago, Newton conducted many important (emeritenxps) _____ with gravity and light. He also developed three important scientific ideas. Newton's First, Second, and Third (wLsa) _____ of (otiMno) _____ describe important (fcsore) _____ and their (ftcsefe) _____ on objects.

ACTIVITY 97   Newton's Laws of Motion

Name:_____

Date:_____

Newton's First Law of Motion says that an object that is not moving will not move, and an object that is moving at a certain rate will keep moving at that same rate until some kind of force acts upon it. This is sometimes called the Law of Inertia. Answer the following questions.

1. If a book is sitting on a table, it will not move unless some force acts on it. Name a force that could act on the book to make it move. _____

    _____

2. If a car is going 40 miles per hour down a road, it will keep going at that speed unless some force acts on it. Name a force that could act on the car to make it speed up, slow down, change direction, or stop. _____

    _____

3. If you are riding in a car traveling at 35 miles per hour and the car stops suddenly, what happens to you? Why? _____

    _____

ACTIVITY 98   Force Equals Mass Times Acceleration: F = ma

Name:_____

Date:_____

Newton's Second Law of Motion says that the rate of movement change depends on the amount of matter in the object (mass), the amount of force applied, and the direction of that force. This is also called the Law of Acceleration. Read each statement. Answer the question.

1. If I push a ball across the ground, it will roll. How could I make it roll faster? _____

    _____

2. If I throw a softball straight from home plate to second base, it will zoom through the air. How could I make it move even faster? _____

    If I threw a basketball instead, would it be faster or slower? Why? _____

    _____

3. Which is harder to kick, a soccer ball or a bowling ball? Why? _____

    _____

4. Which would be easier to push, your dad's car or your little brother's wagon? Why?

    _____

ACTIVITY 99 · Newton's Third Law of Motion

Name: _____

Date: _____

Rockets and cannons follow Newton's Third Law of Motion. So do rowers, skiers, and bumper cars. Fill in the missing letters. Write each word on the line to complete the paragraph.

1. Newton's (T __ __ __ d) _____ Law of Motion says that for every action, there is an equal and (o __ __ o __ i __ e) _____ reaction.
2. This is sometimes called the (L __ __) _____ of Interaction.
3. A rocket takes off because the action of gases escaping out the bottom of the ship causes an equally powerful (a __ __ __ __ n) _____ in the opposite direction.
4. This (r __ __ __ __ __ __ n) _____ pushes the rocket upward.
5. When you blow up a balloon and then release it, air (r __ __ h __ __ g) _____ out will cause the balloon to shoot off in the opposite direction.

Challenge: Explain what happens when you row a canoe or a rowboat. How does this show Newton's Third Law of Motion? _____

_____

ACTIVITY 100 · Newton's Laws of Motion Roundup

Name: _____

Date: _____

Review Isaac Newton's Laws of Motion. Remember, the First Law describes inertia. The Second Law describes acceleration, and the Third Law describes action and reaction. Circle the Law of Motion that defines each example.

1. A tennis ball lies on the ground.
   First Law   Second Law   Third Law
2. A Civil War cannon rolls backward after firing.
   First Law   Second Law   Third Law
3. Two men struggle to push a car across the street while a boy pushes a wagon easily.
   First Law   Second Law   Third Law
4. A rocket, with gases streaming out the rear, lifts off.
   First Law   Second Law   Third Law
5. If a bowling ball and a tennis ball are traveling the same speed, the bowling ball dents the wall and the tennis ball bounces off without causing any harm.
   First Law   Second Law   Third Law
6. A bicycle suddenly hits a rock, but the rider flies over the handlebars.
   First Law   Second Law   Third Law
7. A kayaker pushes back water and his boat zips forward.
   First Law   Second Law   Third Law

ACTIVITY 101 Speed, Velocity, Acceleration, and Momentum

Name:_____

Date:_____

In science, some common words have special meanings. Unscramble the word to match each meaning.

1. T A D I C S N E _____: how far an object has traveled. The distance could be in a circle, and the object could end up where it began.

2. P L A C E N D I E M S T _____: how far an object is from its starting point.

3. E S D P E _____: how fast an object covers distance.

4. O C I V T E L Y _____: how fast an object changes position. If an object changes direction, this changes.

5. C R A T I C L E O A E N _____: speeding up or slowing down or changing direction

6. U T M O M E N M _____: a moving object has this. An object that has more mass or an object that is going faster has more of this than a smaller or slower object. It is harder to stop a school bus than a bicycle because the bus has more of this.

ACTIVITY 102 Friction

Name:_____

Date:_____

Friction is everywhere. Find out about it by filling in the missing words.

| heat | slippery | reduce | rubbing |
| wear | waste | force | |

1. Friction is a _____ of resistance.

2. Friction creates _____.

3. It also causes surfaces to _____ down.

4. People who use complex machines often try to _____ friction.

5. Friction can cause wear and _____ energy.

6. Lubricants such as oil or wax are used to make surfaces more _____.

7. You can experience the effects of friction by _____ your hands together.

ACTIVITY 103 **Streamlining**

Name:_____

Date:_____

Friction is a kind of resistance. If you've ever stood outside in a stiff wind, you have felt air resistance. Friction can occur between solids, liquids, and gases. Streamlining is a special kind of design used to reduce friction and resistance by improving the flow of air or water around an object. Answer each question below.

1. Name four vehicles that are often streamlined. _____

_____

2. Name three advantages of streamlining. _____

_____

3. What is friction between a vehicle and the air called? _____

4. What shape is common in streamlined vehicles? _____

Challenge: On your own paper, draw a streamlined car. Use arrows to show the flow of air.

ACTIVITY 104 **Friction: Good or Bad?**

Name:_____

Date:_____

As you have seen, friction can cause many problems. Friction is not all bad, however. Write the advantages and disadvantages of friction in the correct columns.

wears out machine parts	wastes energy	allows pencils to write
keeps us from slipping when we walk	makes brakes work	causes unwanted heat

Good   Bad

_____   _____

_____   _____

_____   _____

Challenge: On your own paper, write a short science fiction story about what would happen if you woke up one morning and the force friction had disappeared from your town.

ACTIVITY 105 Got Momentum?
Pass It On

Name:_____

Date:_____

When a moving object hits another object, the total momentum of the two objects stays the same. That means that the object that is hit receives momentum from the moving object. This is called conservation of momentum. Write "C" for the examples that conserve momentum, and "NC" for the examples that do not conserve momentum.

1. _____ A blue marble hits a red marble and the red marble rolls.

2. _____ A green bumper car hits an orange bumper car head-on and the green car slows down, while the orange car moves in the opposite direction.

3. _____ A green marble sits on the floor.

4. _____ A boy climbs out of a bumper car after the buzzer rings.

5. _____ In a pool game, the cue ball hits a yellow ball and the yellow ball hits a blue ball.

Challenge: Draw a picture on your own paper showing the conservation of momentum. Use arrows to show force.

ACTIVITY 106 Whoa!
Terminal Velocity

Name:_____

Date:_____

When an object is dropped from a great height, the pull of gravity causes it to accelerate. Because the object is falling through the gases of the atmosphere, air resistance (drag) slows it down. When air resistance balances gravity, the object stops accelerating and falls at a constant (even) speed, which is known as *terminal velocity*. Read each statement and circle true or false. If the statement is false, rewrite the statement to make it true.

1. After a falling skydiver reaches his terminal velocity, he stops in midair. True / False

_____

2. After a falling metal weight reaches its terminal velocity, it falls faster and faster until it reaches the ground. True / False _____

_____

3. When an object is first dropped, its speed increases. True / False _____

_____

4. Terminal velocity for a dropped one-kilogram weight would be the same on every planet and moon in the solar system. True / False _____

_____

ACTIVITY 107 Centripetal Force

Name:_____

Date:_____

Centripetal force pulls an object toward the center of a circle or a sphere. Circle the best choice.

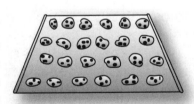

1. According to Newton's First Law of Motion, an object in motion tends to move
   a. in a straight line.   b. in a circle.   c. downwards.

2. The gravity of the earth
   a. is the same as centripetal force.   b. is neutralized by centripetal force.
   c. exerts centripetal force on the moon.

3. If suddenly released from centripetal force, the earth would probably
   a. explode.   b. crash into the sun.   c. move into space on a straight course.

4. When you hit a tetherball, it travels in a circle because of
   a. centripetal force.   b. gravity.   c. the shape of the ball.

5. You are riding in the car when your mom makes a sudden turn. You are pressed against the car door. You have experienced
   a. Newton's First Law of Motion.   b. centrifugal force.   c. centripetal force.

ACTIVITY 108 Elasticity and Plastic Behavior

Name:_____

Date:_____

Forces such as velocity are influenced by an object's mass and sometimes by its size or shape. Many objects cannot change their shape, but some can. The ability of an object to change its shape when force is applied, and then return to its original shape when the force is removed, is called *elasticity*. Some objects do not return to their original shape after force is applied. Instead, they remain in the new shape. This is called *plastic behavior*. Write each example in the correct column.

> clay   trampoline   rubber band   cookie dough
> wet sand   stretch material in a bathing suit

Elasticity   **Plastic Behavior**

_____   _____

_____   _____

_____   _____

ACTIVITY 109   Vibration

Name: _____

Date: _____

Have you ever watched a guitar string after it is plucked? If so, you have seen an example of vibration. A vibration is a special kind of motion. When something vibrates, it moves in a definite repeating pattern. The vibration's frequency describes how often, or frequently, the pattern repeats in one second. The amplitude describes how far a point on the vibrating object moves from its at-rest position. Musical instruments depend on vibration to create their special sounds. Use the clues to unscramble the words.

1. A vibration is a kind of V E M E N M O T _____.
2. Every vibration has a repeating T E N P A R T _____.
3. The number of times a pattern repeats every second is the vibration's F U E N Q Y C R E _____.
4. The farthest distance a vibrating object, such as a guitar string, moves from its at-rest position is the vibration's T U M D E A P L I _____.
5. Musical E N R U M T I N S T S _____ such as drums, violins, and horns use vibration to create their special sounds.

- -

ACTIVITY 110   Waves

Name: _____

Date: _____

You are probably familiar with waves in the ocean or in the local lake. There are also waves inside this room with you right now. Use the word box to complete each sentence. Use a dictionary if you need help.

| Transverse | oscillation | space | Longitudinal |

1. Waves are energy moving through _____.
2. There are two kinds of waves. _____ waves move back and forth at right angles to the energy's direction of travel.
3. _____ waves move back and forth in the energy's direction of travel.
4. A complete back-and-forth movement of either type of wave is called an _____.

Challenge: On your own paper, draw a beach ball riding the top of a transverse wave. Label the direction of travel of the wave and the motion of the ball. Remember, the oscillation will be up and down, but the wave's energy will be heading for the beach.

ACTIVITY 111 Einstein's Special Theory of Relativity

Name:_____

Date:_____

Albert Einstein had some of the greatest scientific insights of our time. Using the words in the box, fill in the blanks.

ground	lightning	thought experiment
observers	time	light motion

1. Albert Einstein thought about _____ and _____.
2. He created a _____.
3. A person on a moving train and a person watching the train go by each saw two bolts of _____ hit two poles exactly a car-length apart.
4. The person on the _____ saw the bolts hit at the same time, but for the person on the train, the pole in the front was hit first, because that light did not have as far to travel.
5. Einstein explained that things that happen at the same time for some observers do not happen at the same time for all _____.
6. He went on to say that for a traveler approaching the speed of light, _____ would slow down.

ACTIVITY 112 Albert Einstein: Warped Space and Masses of Light

Name:_____

Date:_____

After the publication of the Special Theory of Relativity, Einstein realized that his ideas about light, speed, and time did not quite fit Newton's model of gravity. Use the clues to unscramble the words and complete each sentence.

1. Something about Newton's First Law of Motion, the law of E R A I T I N _____, bothered Einstein.
2. He knew that nothing traveled faster than the speed of G H L I T _____.
3. Newton's Law implied that if the sun disappeared, the E T S L A P N _____ would fly off into space right away.
4. Einstein knew that it took about eight minutes for N L U H T I G S _____ to reach Earth. How could gravity travel faster than that? He knew it could not.
5. Einstein created a new model of gravity. He visualized space and time as a four-N N D I M S I O E A L _____ elastic fabric. Large objects, like the sun, made curved dents or warps in this fabric that caused other objects to move around them.
6. His famous equation $E = mc^2$ states that mass is filled with tremendous energy and that energy, including light, has actual A S M A _____.
   (Note: c = the speed of light, and the ^{2} means to multiply that huge number by itself!)

ACTIVITY 113 Motion Roundup

Name:_____

Date:_____

What do you remember about motion?
Shade the circle of the best choice.

1. shows plastic behavior
   - (a.) rubber band
   - (b.) chewing gum
   - (c.) centripetal force

2. force that draws moving objects toward a central point
   - (a.) friction
   - (b.) centrifugal force
   - (c.) centripetal force

3. energy moving through space
   - (a.) waves
   - (b.) terminal velocity
   - (c.) resistance

4. friction between a moving object and the atmosphere
   - (a.) centrifugal force
   - (b.) air resistance
   - (c.) equation

5. things that happen at the same time for some observers do not happen at the same time for all observers
   - (a.) Law of Inertia
   - (b.) Law of Acceleration
   - (c.) Special Theory of Relativity

6. number of times a vibration pattern repeats in a second
   - (a.) oscillation
   - (b.) frequency
   - (c.) amplitude

ACTIVITY 114 Matter and Motion Roundup

Name:_____

Date:_____

What do you remember about matter and motion? Match the correct definition or example to each term.

1. _____ friction
2. _____ terminal velocity
3. _____ acceleration
4. _____ states of matter
5. _____ a crystal
6. _____ an acid
7. _____ creates carbon dioxide
8. _____ the Third Law of Motion
9. _____ fluid
10. _____ a simple machine

a. solid, liquid, gas
b. vinegar
c. resistant force between surfaces of two substances
d. speed at which drag balances the pull of gravity
e. a lever
f. every action has an equal and opposite reaction
g. table salt
h. the carbon cycle
i. speeding up, slowing down, or changing direction
j. a liquid or a gas

ACTIVITY 115   What Is Light?

Name: _____

Date: _____

It has inspired artists and poets. It fascinated
Albert Einstein. It gives life to plants and animals, but what is light? Use the word box to finish
the sentences.

> visible   waves   straight
> electromagnetic   faster

1. Light is one kind of _____ radiation.

2. The light we can see is called _____
    light.

3. Nothing travels _____ than light.

4. Light travels in _____.

5. Light tends to travel in _____ lines.

ACTIVITY 116   Light Waves

Name: _____

Date: _____

Light travels in waves. Find the hidden word in each
group of letters and circle it to find out more about waves. Then write the word on the blank.

1. Like ocean waves, light waves are roixfretransverseblkemnyrea.

    _____

2. Light waves carry energy through xcsoytnmerzspaceiwmbdsqopddg.

    _____

3. Some waves can only move through a fluid or a solid, but light waves can
    move easily through a ydewmblopvacuumiorssdelped.

    _____

4. The brightness or dimness of a light is called its gerttipolmkintensityryus.

    _____

5. As they travel away from their point of origin, light waves uytruenspreadppewmn out.

    _____

Challenge: Write a scientific question about light waves. Include one example of scientific evidence you might use to answer it. _____

_____

ACTIVITY 117   Transparent, Translucent, or Opaque

Name:_____

Date:_____

Light waves can pass easily through some substances. Those substances are transparent. Other substances block light completely. They are opaque. Fog, smoke, textured glass, and tracing paper scatter light. They are translucent. Circle the best word to match each clue.

1. car windshield   transparent   translucent   opaque
2. bathroom ripple glass   transparent   translucent   opaque
3. brick wall   transparent   translucent   opaque
4. lets only light pass through   transparent   translucent   opaque
5. blocks all light   transparent   translucent   opaque
6. tissue paper   transparent   translucent   opaque
7. steel   transparent   translucent   opaque
8. a wooden door   transparent   translucent   opaque
9. plastic sandwich bag   transparent   translucent   opaque

Challenge: Look around the room. List one thing that is transparent, one thing that is translucent, and one thing that is opaque. Which object will cast the darkest shadow? Why?

_____

ACTIVITY 118   Lenses

Name:_____

Date:_____

Lenses are usually made of transparent glass or plastic. They bend, or refract, light to help us see things more clearly. If seen from the side, convex lenses bulge out in the center. They make light rays converge, or come together. The lens in a human eye is a converging, convex lens. Converging lenses make light rays come together and cross over each other. Concave lenses are diverging lenses. If seen from the side, they look caved in. They make light rays diverge, or spread apart. A projector uses a concave lens. Write each clue about lenses in the correct column.

| makes light waves bend outward | human eye | curves inward | converging |
| makes light waves bend inward | projector | bulges outward | diverging |

Convex   **Concave**

_____   _____

_____   _____

_____   _____

_____   _____

ACTIVITY 119 Lasers: Concentrated Light

Name:_____

Date:_____

High-tech lasers help us to point, level, and cut with astonishing precision. The light beams that these devices produce are coherent, which means they stick together as they travel. Find the hidden word in each group of letters and complete each sentence.

1. The light we see, or visible light, contains many different tuwrtylpwavelengthssertmk

   _____.

2. Visible light also contains many different opyuewqfdsfrequenciesspecyum

   _____.

3. Lasers work by using only one wavelength and frequency to create a powerful

   light opytywqlaslibeamvisibdiffwop _____.

4. The first lasers contained a rod made from a synthetic

   eruwsaphmdiamrubysilgogepwv _____.

5. Today's lasers have many different designs and use many different substances to create

   oxvuylkbecoherentfrequnwav _____ light beams.

- -

ACTIVITY 120 Refraction

Name:_____

Date:_____

In space, light rays travel in a straight line at about 186,000 miles per second. When it enters the earth's atmosphere, however, a light ray's speed changes, and often its direction changes, too. Use the word box to complete each sentence.

refraction	slows	density
bent	break	matter

1. Water is thicker and heavier than air because it has more

   _____ per square inch.

2. Scientists say that water has a greater _____ than air.

3. When a light ray comes down through the air and hits water in a glass, it

   _____ down.

4. If the ray enters or leaves the water at an angle, it is also _____,

   or refracted.

5. You can see the effects of _____ when you put a spoon in a

   glass of water and look at it from the side.

6. The spoon seems to _____ in half!

ACTIVITY 121 Lenses Near and Far

Name:_____

Date:_____

Lenses work by refracting light. Combinations of lenses help us see things that are very small or very far away. Read each hint. Circle the best answer about the common uses of lenses.

1. lenses in a tube that help you to see very tiny things

   telescope   microscope   magnifying glass   binoculars   prescription eyeglasses

2. lenses or curved mirrors in a tube that help you see things that are far away

   telescope   microscope   magnifying glass   binoculars   prescription eyeglasses

3. a handheld lens that helps you see details easily

   telescope   microscope   magnifying glass   binoculars   prescription eyeglasses

4. corrects vision nearsightedness, farsightedness, or astigmatism

   telescope   microscope   magnifying glass   binoculars   prescription eyeglasses

5. a pair of small telescopes to help you see wildlife or sporting events

   telescope   microscope   magnifying glass   binoculars   prescription eyeglasses

---

ACTIVITY 122 Reflection

Name:_____

Date:_____

Everyone knows what a reflection is, but what causes it? Use the word box to finish each sentence.

| reflected | shiny | regular | different |
| diffuse | incident | angle | |

1. When parallel rays of light are traveling toward a surface or an object, they are called _____ rays.

2. Light rays that bounce off of any surface are called _____ rays.

3. If a light ray hits the surface of a mirror at a certain _____, it will bounce off the surface at exactly the same angle, like a ball after striking the backstop.

4. When reflected rays travel in paths that stay parallel, it is a _____ reflection.

5. When incident rays hit rough, choppy water, each ray hits the water surface differently, and so each is reflected at a _____ angle.

6. When reflected rays go off in many directions, it is called a _____ reflection.

7. Only smooth, _____ surfaces produce regular reflections.

ACTIVITY 123 Cameras and Projectors   Name:_____

Date:_____

Cameras are tools for capturing images. Projectors make images larger so they can be shared with a group. Both cameras and projectors use lenses to refract light. Unscramble the letters to complete each sentence.

1. Cameras use lenses to refract light and O F S C U

   _____ images on a piece of film or a sensor.

2. Once, all cameras used a chemical reaction to store information about

   light on L M I F _____.

3. Today, most people use I T D A L I G _____ cameras, which use

   sensors to capture and record details about light and color as a series of numbers.

4. When a speaker or a teacher wants to show pictures to a large group of people, he uses

   a R O J E O P C T R _____.

5. There are many kinds of projectors, but they all use N C O A V C E

   _____ lenses to spread out light rays and make images fill the

   screen.

ACTIVITY 124 Prisms and Visible Light   Name:_____

Date:_____

Have you ever placed a glass prism in a window and watched a rainbow appear? If so, you have seen the spectrum of visible light. Circle the hidden word in each group of letters to complete each sentence.

1. Visible white light contains many different tuwrqsddwavelengthspdyubymnb.
2. Each wavelength of the visible spectrum is a different trewicxssgjiocolormkp.
3. A rainbow appears when sunlight shines through raindrops and the drops break retybbnmdwhiteplozcblyr light into its colors.
4. You do not have to wait for a storm to see a rainbow. Specially cut pieces of glass and crystal can also reveal the colors in white light. A triangular piece of glass designed to break up light is called a bbernntssieyprismpprbckldqp.
5. Colors you can see in a rainbow include red, orange, yellow, green, blue, indigo, and powtllqxzvioletmnnght.
6. When an object appears to be a certain color, it is because that object is absorbing (soaking up) all of the other wavelengths in white light and tobbydreflectingjkbxwppi only that one color back to our eyes.
7. When an apple appears red, its skin is absorbing all of the colors rypottexceptmswyazlx red, which it reflects.

ACTIVITY 125 The Spectrum Human Eyes Can't Detect

Name:_____

Date:_____

The colors we see—the visible spectrum—are only part of the electromagnetic spectrum. Sunlight contains other wavelengths our eyes cannot see, but we can experience them in other ways. Some of these invisible wavelengths are on the red side of the visible spectrum. We experience infrared rays as heat. Beyond infrared are rays with even longer wavelengths. They include microwaves and radio waves. Ultraviolet rays, which can cause skin and eye damage, have shorter wavelengths than violet light. Beyond them are X-rays and gamma rays.

1. The visible spectrum is part of a larger spectrum. What is it? _____

    _____

2. Which wavelengths are beyond red on the red end of the visible spectrum? _____

    _____

3. Which wavelengths are beyond violet on the violet end of the visible spectrum?_____

    _____

4. Name four other invisible wavelengths in the electromagnetic spectrum. _____

    _____

ACTIVITY 126 Ultraviolet Light

Name:_____

Date:_____

Are invisible rays attacking your skin every time you go to the beach? Do the exercise and find out about this notorious part of the electromagnetic spectrum. Fill in the missing letters and then write the word on the line.

1. Ultraviolet light has a wavelength that is slightly (sh __ __ t __ r) than visible violet light. _____

2. Even though we can't see them, ultraviolet rays are part of (s __ __ li __ __ t). _____

3. Our skin and (ti __ __ u __ s) in our eyes are sensitive to ultraviolet rays.

    _____

4. Ultraviolet light does have practical uses. Special symbols only visible with ultraviolet light are used to help merchants spot (f __ __ __) credit cards. _____

5. Traps with a deep purple glow are used to kill small flying (in __ __ __ __ __), because certain bugs are attracted to ultraviolet light. _____

6. Ultraviolet radiation is also being used as part of the (p __ r __ fic __ t __ __ n) process for city drinking water. _____

ACTIVITY 127   **Infrared Light**

Name:_____

Date:_____

You can't see them, but you probably know when these rays are around. Complete this exercise and learn more about this invisible part of the spectrum.

1. Infrared rays have _____ wavelengths than visible red light
   a. shorter   b. longer   c. more powerful
2. Most infrared waves are invisible, but they are often sensed by _____.
   a. your ears   b. your tongue   c. temperature sensors in your skin
3. In a spacecraft's cooling system, the heat energy transferred by _____ is carried by infrared waves.
   a. radiation   b. convection   c. conduction
4. About half of the _____ we receive from the sun is carried by infrared waves.
   a. magnetism   b. heat   c. cancer
5. Infrared waves that are very close to waves we can see are often used, with special cameras, in _____ equipment.
   a. night vision   b. stereo   c. magnetic

ACTIVITY 128   **A Short History of Artificial Lighting**

Name:_____

Date:_____

The ability to control light and enjoy it at night has been important to the development of modern civilization. Find a hidden word in each group of letters to complete each sentence. Write it on the line.

1. The first artificial light was a uylkelewtricfirerepn. _____
2. People quickly learned how to carry light from place to place using yrwtorchesnsffit. _____
3. Early lamps were made from hollowed-out rock and burned animal losmfatrdcche. _____
4. Later, candles and oil-burning prdwolanternsshytel made indoor lighting safer, easier, and more efficient. _____
5. Thomas Edison's electric light rewsstbulbsnsfpekl, similar to incandescent lights still used today, were first produced in 1880. _____
6. Bulbs that ceuiconvertoutmls energy into more light and less heat, such as light emitting diodes (LEDs) and fluorescent tubes, are replacing incandescent lights in many homes and businesses. _____

ACTIVITY 129   Movies and Animation

Name:_____

Date:_____

Moving pictures, whether they are photographed with a movie camera or drawn by hand, are actually a kind of trick, or illusion. Find out more about movies by completing this activity. Circle the best choice.

1. Movies are really a series of _____ pictures called frames.
   a. ultraviolet   b. three-dimensional   c. still

2. Each frame stays on the screen for between 1/24 and 1/30 of a _____.
   a. second   b. hour   c. year

3. The actors in a series of movie frames seem to _____ because our eyes and brains take time to process the information in a scene.
   a. sing   b. disappear   c. move

4. This phenomenon is called persistence of _____.
   a. hearing   b. drama   c. vision

5. Live-action movie frames are recorded with cameras, while cartoon frames begin with _____.
   a. drawings or other artwork   b. sound recordings   c. television images

6. Today, both live action films and cartoon features use _____ technology.
   a. obsolete   b. digital   c. ultraviolet

ACTIVITY 130   Optical Illusions

Name:_____

Date:_____

Motion pictures are not the only kind of visual trick. Can you spot the illusions?

1. Which horizontal line at right is longer, a or b?
   _____

2. Which line at right is longer, c or d?
   _____

3. Which gray square at right is darker, e or f?
   _____

4. Which way are the horizontal lines at right tilting?
   _____

ACTIVITY 131 Light Roundup

Name:_____

Date:_____

Find out what you have learned about light by matching.

1. _____ persistence of vision
2. _____ visible spectrum
3. _____ infrared light
4. _____ frequency
5. _____ wave

6. _____ green
7. _____ convex lens
8. _____ refraction

a. number of times an oscillation repeats per second
b. the bending of light rays
c. energy moving through space
d. part of the electromagnetic spectrum we can see
e. electromagnetic rays slightly longer than visible red light
f. phenomenon that makes animation work
g. seen when an object absorbs all colors except green
h. thicker in the center than at the edges

ACTIVITY 132 Light Roundup

Name:_____

Date:_____

Find out what you have learned about light by shading the correct circle.

1. A movie frame is a _____ picture.
   a. moving   b. still   c. black and white
2. Invisible light waves that can cause sunburns are _____.
   a. rare   b. infrared   c. ultraviolet
3. Lightbulbs were first manufactured in _____.
   a. 1860   b. 1905   c. 1880
4. Optical illusions prove that your sense of sight _____.
   a. should always be trusted   b. has limitations   c. is the most important sense
5. The electromagnetic spectrum _____.
   a. is part of the visible spectrum   b. includes X-rays   c. contains no waves
6. Lasers create _____.
   a. coherent light beams   b. prisms   c. convection currents
7. A banana is yellow because its skin absorbs every color except _____.
   a. purple   b. green   c. yellow

ACTIVITY 133   Sound Waves

Name:_____

Date:_____

     Sound waves are different from light waves in some important ways. Sound waves are mechanical waves. Electromagnetic waves can move easily through the vacuum of space. Sound cannot travel in outer space. Sound can only travel through gases, liquids, and solids. Sound waves are compression waves. That means they travel by pushing molecules together like a pressed spring. A sound wave's compression journey begins with a vibrating object. Sound waves move out in all directions like the ones that spread after a pebble is thrown in a pond. Like light, sound can travel in high, medium, or low-frequency waves.

1.   Why is space silent? _____

2.   How do compression waves travel? _____

3.   How do sound waves begin? _____

4.   How are sound waves like waves in a pond? _____

Challenge: Create a scientific question about sound waves. Include an example of scientific

evidence you might use to answer the question. _____

_____

- -

ACTIVITY 134   The Speed of Sound

Name:_____

Date:_____

     If light and sound waves had a race, which would win? Complete the activity to find out.

water	Thunder	speed
slowly	farther	temperatures

1.   Sound waves travel much more _____ than light waves.

2.   Sound waves move more slowly at low _____.

3.   Surprisingly, sound waves move more quickly through _____ than air.

4.   Low-frequency sound waves travel _____ than high-frequency waves.

5.   When an accelerating jet catches up with and passes the _____ of sound, it creates the loud noise we call a sonic boom.

6.   _____ and lightning happen at the same time, but the boom reaches you later because sound is much slower than light.

ACTIVITY 135 Loudness

Name: _____

Date: _____

The volume of a note describes how loud or soft it sounds. Fill in the missing letters in each word and then write the word on the line.

1. Some sounds are very (l __ __ d) and others are soft. _____

2. The energy contained in a sound wave is its (i __ te __ si __ y). _____

3. The (l __ __ dn __ __ s) of a particular sound is a perception and is different for every person. For example, television volume that is too loud for a teenager might not be loud enough for her grandmother. _____

4. A sound has the greatest amplitude near its (s __ __ __ ce). _____

5. The amplitude (loudness) of a sound is measured in (d __ __ ib __ ls). _____

6. Complete (s __ l __ n __ e) measures at zero decibels. _____

7. (W __ __ le) songs have been measured at between 155 and 188 decibels. _____

8. Sounds at 120 decibels are so loud they hurt your (e __ __ __ __). _____

ACTIVITY 136 Pitch

Name: _____

Date: _____

The pitch of a note describes how high or low it sounds. Use the word box to fill in the blanks.

infrasound	earthquake	vibrate	ultrasound
dolphins	frequency	oscillations	

1. Sounds can be high, like a bird's song, or low, like the rumble of an _____.

2. A high-pitched sound comes from high-_____ waves.

3. Remember, the frequency of any wave measures how many complete _____ there are per second.

4. Things that _____ very slowly create low-pitched sounds.

5. Frequencies above our hearing range are called _____.

6. Frequencies below our hearing range are called _____.

7. The clicks _____ use to navigate through murky ocean waters are ultrasonic.

ACTIVITY 137 Resonance

Name:_____

Date:_____

Resonance gives guitars and other instruments their rich sounds. Find the hidden word in each group of letters and write it on the line.

1. Each object has its own tyurwresonantxcvr frequency. _____

2. If you have ever swung really high on a playground rewuqzswingpoyzx, you know that the swing works best at a certain speed and height. _____

3. In sound, an object's resonant frequency is the pitch at which it puyqzvibratesdfsnbie the most powerfully. _____

4. Some wine glasses resonate so strongly when a masterful opera singer holds a particular note that they powtmbshatterdsuyr. _____

5. Resonance depends on many factors. For example, small glasses resonate at poyrmnhigherdsrslmn frequencies than larger glasses. _____

ACTIVITY 138 Amplification

Name:_____

Date:_____

Hey! Can you hear me? Shade the circle of the best choice to find out how performers make themselves heard.

1. Speakers and performers want the _____ to hear them.
   (a.) microphones   (b.) stadium   (c.) audience
2. Speakers use _____ to make their voices sound loud and clear.
   (a.) microphones   (b.) vibrations   (c.) ultrasound
3. Rock and country musicians depend on _____ to make the sounds of their guitars fill a stadium.
   (a.) vibrations   (b.) infrasound   (c.) amplifiers
4. Microphones and loudspeakers use _____ to increase the power of sound waves.
   (a.) ultrasound   (b.) electromagnetism (c.) echoes
5. A cello's wooden body resonates and _____ the sounds created by the instrument's vibrating strings.
   (a.) deadens   (b.) shatters   (c.) amplifies

ACTIVITY 139   Echoes

Name:_____

Date:_____

Hello! Hello! Hello! Use the word box to fill in the blanks to find out more about echoes.

```
reflected      navigation      source
bounce         echolocation
```

1. Echoes happen when sound waves _____ off of a surface.
2. An echo is a _____ sound wave.
3. The farther away the reflective surface is from the sound _____, the longer the echo will take to return.
4. Bats and dolphins use _____ to help them navigate in low light.
5. Sonar stands for "sound _____ rang-ing." It uses echoes to locate objects in the ocean depths.

ACTIVITY 140   Sound Absorption

Name:_____

Date:_____

Sometimes, silence is important. Unscramble the letters to find out how sound engineers control distracting noise.

1. Some materials (fterlce) sound. _____
2. Other materials (orbasb) sound. _____
3. Soft materials are used on the walls, floors, and ceilings of restaurants to (olcntro) noise levels. _____
4. Outdoors, trees and large bushes planted near roads can soak up (aficftr) noise. _____
5. Music practice rooms are often (oofeusondprd) with soft, insulating tiles. _____
6. Designers of concert halls study (uicsacots) to give audiences the best experiences possible. _____

Challenge: Write a scientific question about sound reflection (echoes) and sound absorption.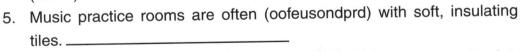
Include one type of evidence you might use to answer it.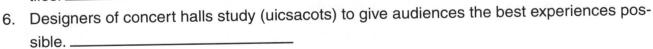

ACTIVITY 141 Sound Reproduction

Name:_____

Date:_____

Everyone listens to recorded music. Fill in the missing letters to find out more about it.

1. In digital recordings, sounds are sampled and c __ nv __ __ t __ d to a series of numbers.

2. In a high fidelity recording, the sound is s __ __ pl __ d more than 40,000 times per second.

3. A d __ g __ t __ l recording can be played thousands of times, and the sound stays the same because the numbers do not change.

4. The only numbers digital recordings use are zero and one. This is called a b __ __ __ y code.

5. The digital code is stored on the shiny side of a c __ __ p __ __ t disc (CD) and is read by a laser beam.

6. An MP3 player is another way of l __ __ t __ __ ing to a digital recording.

ACTIVITY 142 Sound Roundup

Name:_____

Date:_____

How much do you remember about sound? Find out with this matching activity.

1. _____ reflection
2. _____ absorption
3. _____ binary code
4. _____ amplification
5. _____ resonance
6. _____ pitch
7. _____ ultrasound
8. _____ decibels

a. soaking up
b. bouncing off, echoes
c. units that measure loudness of sound
d. highness or lowness of a note
e. a sound above the human range of hearing
f. a two-number code used in digital recording
g. making sounds loud enough to be heard
h. a natural vibration frequency; different for every object

10011010001101010

ACTIVITY 143 Flight

Name: _____

Date: _____

Since ancient times, people have watched soaring birds and longed to fly. In 1783, two brothers, Joseph and Jacques Montgolfier, built the first successful hot air balloon. In 1903, brothers Orville and Wilbur Wright flew the first successful heavier-than-air craft. Today, lighter-than-air craft such as blimps sometimes hover over football games, and hot-air ballooning is a popular hobby, but most planes are heavier than air. Place the words in the column with which they are associated.

Joseph and Jacques Montgolfier	airplane	blimp	helium airship
Orville and Wilbur Wright	helicopter	balloon	passenger jet

Lighter than Air   **Heavier than Air**

_____   _____

_____   _____

_____   _____

_____   _____

ACTIVITY 144 Lift

Name: _____

Date: _____

How does a heavy plane get off the ground? Fill in the blanks to find out.

pressure	drag	curved	faster
thrust	denser	airfoil	engines

1. The shape of a plane's wing is an _____.

2. The upper surface of the wing is _____.

3. Because it has to go farther in the same length of time, air flows _____ over the curved upper surface than it does over the wing's flat bottom.

4. The fast-moving air above the wing has less _____ than the slower-moving air underneath.

5. The slower, _____ air moving under the wings causes the plane to rise. This is called lift.

6. The bodies of planes are streamlined to overcome air resistance, or _____.

7. The power or force that makes a plane move forward in the air is called _____.

8. Large jet _____ provide the thrust for modern passenger planes.

ACTIVITY 145 Displacement

Name:_____

Date:_____

What happens to the water when you jump in the pool? Fill in the missing letters to answer the questions.

1. There is a story about a Greek thinker named (A __ ch __ m __ des) who lived about 2,300 years ago.

2. One day, he was climbing into his (b __ __ h). He noticed that the level of the water rose and sloshed over the edge when he sat down in it.

3. Archimedes realized that he had pushed some of the (w __ __ __ __) out of the way to make room for his body.

Archimedes

4. When an object is placed in a (f __ __ __ d), it displaces some of that fluid, or moves it aside.

5. When ships float, they (di __ __ __ __ ce) some of the water under them.

6. When hot-air or helium balloons (f __ __ __ t), they displace some of the air above them.

ACTIVITY 146 Buoyancy

Name:_____

Date:_____

When an object displaces water or air, it will either float or sink. Archimedes' principle says that the *upthrust* on an object in a fluid is equal to the weight of the fluid it *displaces*. When you put a block of wood in water, it will keep sinking until the upthrust under the wood equals its weight. If you put a big piece of heavy wood in a wading pool, it might sink because the shallow water would not create enough upthrust. The ability of an object to float is called its *buoyancy*. Write each item in the correct column.

| a ping-pong ball | a coin | a wood pencil | a paper clip |
| an empty bottle with a lid | fingernail clippers | a marshmallow | a ball of clay |

Floats in a Basin of Water

_____

_____

_____

_____

Doesn't Float in a Basin of Water

_____

_____

_____

_____

Challenge: On your own paper, draw a rubber duck in a bathtub. Label the displacement and the upthrust.

ACTIVITY 147 What Is an Atom?

Name:_____

Date:_____

It is hard to imagine how small atoms are. This page could be almost a million atoms thick. Unscramble each word and write it on the line.

1. The Greeks believed that all (tatemr) _____ could be divided into tiny parts.
2. A scientist named John Dalton later named those tiny parts atoms, using the Greek word for (iisiivblnde) _____.
3. We now know that (tomsa) _____ are not indivisible.
4. They consist of smaller (erticpals) _____.
5. Although they are composed of smaller particles, atoms are the smallest bits of an element that have the (popiesertr) _____ of that element.
6. An iron atom is the (msallest) _____ bit of iron that is still iron.
7. Two thousand years ago, the Greeks had no way to prove the (isteeencx) _____ of atoms.
8. Today, scientists can photograph atoms using electron (osrescopmic) _____.

ACTIVITY 148 Structure of the Atom

Name:_____

Date:_____

It is useful to think of the atom as a group of protons and neutrons in a nucleus, or center, with electrons circling around them. This is not how an atom really looks. It is a scientific model of an atom. Scientists are learning more about the structure of the atom every year. For example, they have discovered that protons and neutrons are composed of even smaller particles called quarks. Match the correct definition to the word.

1. _____ atom
2. _____ nucleus
3. _____ charge
4. _____ proton
5. _____ quark
6. _____ neutron
7. _____ electron

a. part of the nucleus with neither a positive nor negative charge
b. protons and neutrons are made of these tiny particles
c. smallest unit of matter that has the properties of a particular element
d. center of an atom
e. orbits the nucleus and has a negative charge
f. part of the nucleus that has a positive charge
g. positive or negative

ACTIVITY 149 Structure of the Molecule

Name:_____

Date:_____

Atoms join together to make molecules of elements and compounds. Fill in the missing letters to complete the words. Write each word on the line.

1. Atoms build m __ __ __ __ r by joining together with other atoms. _____

2. If an atom joins with another atom of the same e __ __ __ __ nt, it forms a molecule of that element. _____

3. For example, two o __ __ __ e __ atoms can join together. _____

4. Two oxygen atoms make a m __ l __ c __ le of the element oxygen. _____

5. If atoms of different elements join together, they form a molecule of a

   c __ __ p __ __ nd. _____

6. For example, two h __ __ __ og __ n atoms often join with one oxygen atom. _____

7. They form a molecule of the compound w __ __ __ r. _____

ACTIVITY 150 Molecules

Name:_____

Date:_____

Remember, atoms of the same element create a molecule of that element. Atoms of different elements combine to create a molecule of a compound. Write each molecule name in the correct column. The atoms in each molecule are included to help you decide.

oxygen (2 atoms of oxygen)

rust (1 atom of iron and 2 atoms of oxygen)

table salt (1 atom of sodium and 1 atom of chlorine)

water (2 atoms of hydrogen and 1 atom of oxygen)

nitrogen (2 atoms of nitrogen)

hydrogen (2 atoms of hydrogen)

Molecules of Elements	Molecules of Compounds
_____	_____
_____	_____
_____	_____

ACTIVITY 151 **History of the Periodic Table**   Name:_____

Date:_____

The Periodic Table is a chart that helps scientists understand the elements. Use the word box to fill in the blanks.

Mendeleyev

electricity	substances	Periodic	chart	elements
predicted	isolate	Dmitri	chlorine	compounds

Elements are the building blocks of _____. They

are pure _____. Some _____,

such as copper, gold, and silver, are sometimes found in a pure state. Other elements, such as

sodium and _____, have to be broken down from compounds. In the 1700s

and 1800s, discoveries in _____ and light made it possible for scientists

to _____ elements never before seen in their pure state. In 1869, Rus-

sian scientist _____ Mendeleyev created a _____

that organized all of the known elements and _____ elements that had

not yet been discovered. It was called the _____ Table.

ACTIVITY 152 **Structure of the Periodic Table**   Name:_____

Date:_____

The Periodic Table's power lies in its grouping of elements and its logical progression from simple atomic structures to more complex ones. Unscramble each word and write it on the line.

1
H
Hydrogen
1.0079

1. The Periodic Table lists every (emteeln) _____.
2. The elements are listed in order according to their atomic (unrmbes) _____.
3. The number of (oprnsto) _____ in an element's nucleus is its atomic number.
4. The columns in the (riodPeic) _____ Table are called groups.
5. The (oswr) _____ in the Periodic Table are called periods.
6. On the table, elements with (marilsi) _____ properties are grouped together.
7. (ourpGs) _____ of elements on the table have names.
8. A few of these groups are metals, (mentalons) _____, and transition metals.
9. Each of the elements has a symbol. For example, (ydrohgen) _____ is H and its atomic number is 1.

ACTIVITY 153 Discovery of
Radioactivity

Name:_____

Date:_____

Radioactive materials have changed our world. Use the word box to fill in the blanks.

| strange | cancer | stable | radium | chemistry | Geiger | uranium |

1. In the late 1800s and early 1900s, scientists explored the _____ properties of certain compounds.
2. In 1896, Antoine Becquerel discovered that a _____ compound could fog photographic film that was still sealed in its lightproof wrapper.
3. Marie and Pierre Curie started exploring this phenomenon, and in 1902, they isolated plutonium and _____.
4. Unfortunately, the couple did not realize that rays from these elements could cause _____. Marie later died of leukemia.
5. Simultaneously, Ernest Rutherford discovered that radioactive elements threw off alpha or beta radiation before becoming _____.
6. In 1907, Rutherford, along with Hans _____, designed a model of the atom that included a nucleus and circling electrons.
7. He received the 1908 Nobel Prize in _____ for his work.

Curie

ACTIVITY 154 What Is Radioactivity?
E = mc²

Name:_____

Date:_____

In 1915, Albert Einstein took the work of Rutherford and others further. He wrote a paper in which he explained that mass, time, and energy were all, in some ways, related. In fact, he said, mass could be changed to energy and energy could be changed to mass. Huge amounts of power were locked in the bonds that held neutrons and protons together in the nucleus of the tiny atom. This power, he believed, was locked in every atom, but most protons and neutrons were so tightly held that they could not be separated. Scientists soon understood that unstable radioactive atoms might be split apart to release the energy locked in their bonds.

1. What does the letter **m** stand for in Einstein's equation? _____
2. What does the letter **E** stand for in Einstein's equation? _____
3. The letter **c²** stands for the speed of light multiplied by itself. Would **m** times that number be a large amount or a small amount? _____
4. Why are radioactive elements used to generate nuclear energy if the nuclei in all atoms contain this power? _____
5. During World War II, something was created using this power. What was it? _____

_____

ACTIVITY 155 A Tale of Two Particles and Some Waves

Name:_____

Date:_____

There are three types of radiation. These three types of radiation are emitted, or sent out, from unstable atoms. Alpha particles come from the nucleus of an atom. Each one is exactly like the nucleus of a helium atom. Beta particles are electrons ejected from a decaying neutron in the nucleus. They move almost at the speed of light. Gamma rays are not particles. They are part of the electromagnetic spectrum. They are emitted as powerful, dangerous energy after alpha or beta particles are thrown off.

1. Name three types of radiation given off by an unstable compound or element. _____
   _____

2. What are gamma rays? _____
   _____
   _____

3. Which type of radiation contains particles similar to helium atoms? _____

4. How fast do gamma rays travel? _____

ACTIVITY 156 Uses of Radioactivity

Name:_____

Date:_____

Radioactivity can cause illness and even death, but it can also help to cure disease. Fill in the missing letters and write the word on the blank.

1. Radiation treatment is used to kill (c __ __ __ __ r) cells.
   _____

2. Tracers, or small amounts of (r __ d __ __ ac __ __ ve) substances, are injected into patients' bodies so doctors can pinpoint where problems are taking place. _____

3. X-rays are used by doctors and dentists to spot (b __ o __ __ n) bones and other problems inside the body. _____

4. Food suppliers (ir __ __ d __ __ te) food to kill germs and keep food safe. _____

5. Historians use the rate that carbon-14 decays to date (a __ __ if __ __ ts) from ancient civilizations. _____

ACTIVITY 157 Fission, Fusion, and
Nuclear Power

Name:_____

Date:_____

How does nuclear power work? Use the word box to fill in the blanks.

fusion	fission	unstable
waste	nuclear	electricity

1. There are about 100 _____ power plants in the United States.
2. The world gets about 17% of its _____ from nuclear power.
3. Nuclear power plants work by using nuclear _____.
4. They release power by splitting the nuclei of
_____ atoms in a controlled
chain reaction.
5. The joining together of two small atoms also produces
energy. It is called _____.
6. Fusion does not use radioactive materials, and it does not
produce nuclear _____, but
scientists have not yet been able to build a practical power plant based on fusion.

ACTIVITY 158 Atomic Roundup

Name:_____

Date:_____

Find out how much you remember about the atom
by matching the definition to the word.

1. _____ fission
2. _____ alpha particles
3. _____ Marie Curie
4. _____ Periodic Table
5. _____ particles in the nucleus
6. _____ molecule of a compound
7. _____ periods

a. a chart showing all of the elements
b. scientist who helped to isolate radium
c. breaking atoms apart to release energy
d. particles like helium nuclei; released from
unstable atoms
e. rows in the Periodic Table
f. protons and neutrons
g. contains atoms of two or
more different elements

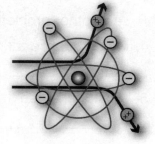

ACTIVITY 159 Renewable and Nonrenewable Power Sources

Name:_____

Date:_____

There is a limited supply of nonrenewable power sources on Earth. Once coal, oil, and natural gas supplies are used up, they will be gone forever. Renewable power supplies are different. They are unlimited. Write each of the renewable and nonrenewable power sources in the correct column.

| geothermal | solar | coal | oil |
| natural gas | tidal | wind | hydroelectric |

Renewable

_____
_____
_____
_____
_____

Nonrenewable

_____
_____
_____

ACTIVITY 160 Recycling

Name:_____

Date:_____

Many things we throw away can be processed and used in different ways. This process is called *recycling*. Unscramble the words and write them on the line to complete the paragraph.

There is a 1. (mditeli) _____ supply of coal, oil, and gas. There is

also a limited amount of 2. (minmaluu) _____, tin, steel, copper, silver,

and other important minerals. Reusing or recycling these 3. (esousrerc) _____

can make them last for a long time. Recycling can save 4. (nergey) _____,

too. Anything made out of 5. (lseet) _____ can be recycled.

Newspapers, aluminum soda cans, glass, and

6. (casplti) _____ drink

bottles can also be recycled.

ACTIVITY 161 Utilizing Resources

Name:_____

Date:_____

The earth has limited resources. How can we better use what we've got? Write your answers in complete sentences on the lines below.

1. Give two reasons why resources should be conserved. _____
   _____

2. Name three ways to save gasoline. _____
   _____

3. Name three ways to save electricity. _____
   _____

4. Name two other natural resources that should be conserved. _____
   _____

5. Name two problems with technological development. _____
   _____

6. Name two things you would like to see invented that would conserve natural resources while maintaining or improving our quality of life. Use your imagination. _____
   _____

ACTIVITY 162 Thinkers Who Shaped Our View of the World

Name:_____

Date:_____

Thousands of fascinating people have devoted their curiosity and diligence to scientific exploration. Each thinker and observer has used the ideas and observations of others as a starting place for fresh questions about what is really happening in the natural world. These exercises have introduced only a few of these people. You can discover many more on the Web and in the library. Circle the scientist who made the following discoveries.

Galileo

1. Three Laws of Motion	Newton	Einstein	Galileo
2. Theory of Relativity	Newton	Einstein	Galileo
3. radioactivity	Einstein	Curie	Tesla
4. alternating current	Galileo	Curie	Tesla
5. Laws of Falling Bodies (objects)	Galileo	Curie	Tesla

Curie

ACTIVITY 163 In the Works: Developing Technologies

Name:_____

Date:_____

Technology is science in action. Scientists are exploring new ideas right now. Some of the inventions that result from these ideas are already being used; others are still in planning stages. Find the hidden word or phrase in each group of letters and write it on the line.

1. A fuel source for cars that produces no emissions:

   ryhswdrohydrogenopnmwl   _____

2. The use of machines to perform tasks by remote control:

   ioeputwxroboticspywqz   _____

3. Extremely tiny motors that run directly on sunlight:

   urewphnanomotorsfwlphe   _____

4. Computer-generated simulated experiences using real actions such as walking:

   prwsfvirtualprealitypsn   _____ _____

5. Energy efficient light panels in the walls and ceilings of buildings:

   prtylightkemittingldiodesptrm   _____ _____ _____

6. For children in countries where electricity is undependable:

   yresdhcheapwind-upolaptopspwqazx _____ _____ _____

ACTIVITY 164 What Makes It Work?

Name:_____

Date:_____

What do all of these laws and theories mean in everyday life? Use what you have learned to complete the exercise by matching.

1. _____ clothes dryer

2. _____ recycling metal sorter

3. _____ laser

4. _____ optical microscope

5. _____ nuclear power

6. _____ construction crane

7. _____ paddling a canoe

8. _____ toaster

9. _____ pencils and erasers

a. coherent light

b. Newton's Third Law of Motion (action/reaction)

c. electrical resistance

d. friction

e. magnetism

f. convection

g. $E = mc^2$

h. refraction

i. simple machine, a pulley

ACTIVITY 165 Using Scientific Ideas

Name:_____

Date:_____

You have learned about many different kinds of
scientific ideas. Review them with this matching exercise.

1. _____ theory
2. _____ model
3. _____ law
4. _____ hypothesis
5. _____ observation
6. _____ evidence
7. _____ definition
8. _____ focused

a. using the senses to gather information
b. an agreed-upon scientific meaning for a term
c. proof; for example, observation, calculation, or experimentation
d. a working mental picture; known to be an approximation
e. narrowed-in on a particular topic; not too general
f. a limited statement about a possible cause and effect relationship
g. established idea that supports a group of other proven ideas
h. established idea; can only be overturned by powerful evidence

ACTIVITY 166 Physical Sciences Vocabulary Roundup

Name:_____

Date:_____

You have learned the special meanings of many scientific terms.
Review them with this matching exercise.

1. _____ work
2. _____ wave
3. _____ energy
4. _____ machine
5. _____ states of matter
6. _____ heat
7. _____ base
8. _____ distance
9. _____ acceleration

a. a device that transmits or modifies energy
b. a substance that neutralizes an acid
c. speeding up, slowing down, or changing direction
d. amount of space traveled
e. energy moving through space
f. the ability to do work, measured in joules
g. solid, liquid, and gas
h. a form of energy that flows from warmer to cooler places
i. energy transmitted by force over a distance

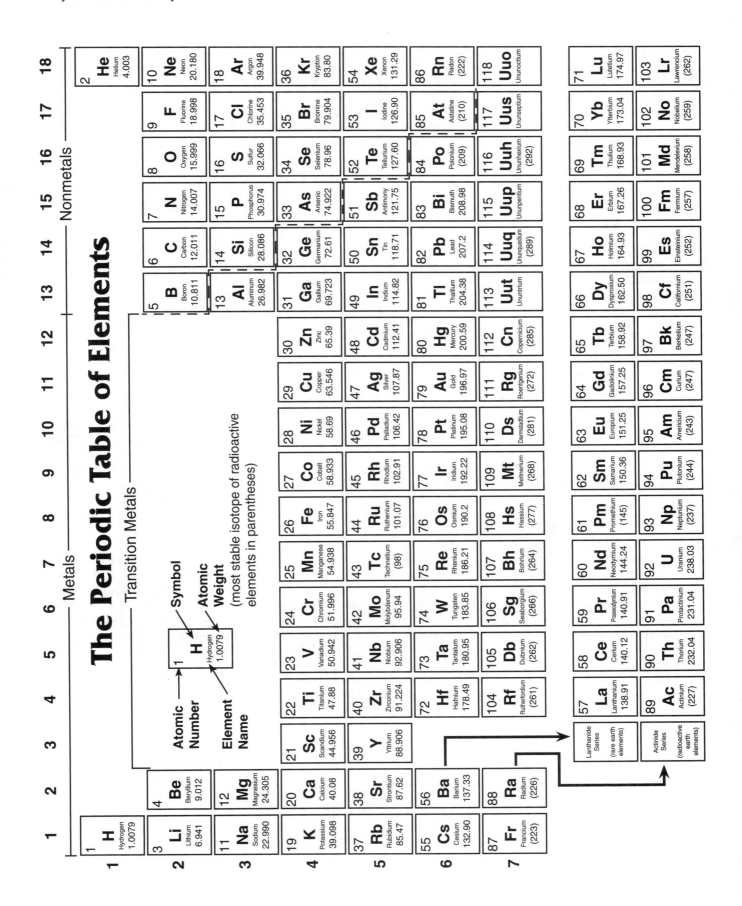

The Periodic Table of Elements

Answer Keys

Answers to all Challenge Questions will vary.

Activity 1 (p. 2)
1. scientific 　　2. non-scientific
3. scientific 　　4. non-scientific

Activity 2 (p. 2)
1. non-focused 　　2. focused
3. non-focused 　　4. focused

Activity 3 (p. 3)
1. a 　　2. a 　　3. a, b 　　4. a

Activity 4 (p. 3)
Answers may vary. All answers may include observation, mathematical calculation, experimentation, and research.

Activity 5 (p. 4)
Answers will vary, but may include:
1. flatten out 　　2. melt
3. torn or wadded up, but not burned
4. evaporate 　　5. wear out or go flat

Activity 6 (p. 4)
Physical Change: shredding junk mail, cutting glass to fix a window, boiling water in a kettle
Chemical Change: burning coal in a power plant, burning wood in a campfire, an egg cooking

Activity 7 (p. 5)
Solid: wood, chalk, cement, glass, steel
Liquid: milk, lemonade, orange juice, dish soap, mouthwash

Activity 8 (p. 5)
1. gas 　　2. solid 　　3. solid 　　4. solid
5. gas 　　6. liquid 　　7. liquid 　　8. liquid
9. liquid 　　10. liquid 　　11. solid 　　12. solid

Activity 9 (p. 6)
1. False 　　2. False 　　3. True 　　4. True

Activity 10 (p. 6)
1. diffusion 　　2. diffusion 　　3. not diffusion
4. diffusion 　　5. Answers will vary.

Activity 11 (p. 7)
1. fluid 　　2. pour 　　3. container
4. solid 　　5. gas 　　6. states

Activity 12 (p. 7)
1. surface tension 　　2. not surface tension
3. not surface tension 　　4. surface tension
5. surface tension

Activity 13 (p. 8)
1. False 　　2. True 　　3. True
4. True 　　5. True

Activity 14 (p. 8)
1. gas to liquid 　　2. solid to liquid 　　3. liquid to gas
4. liquid to solid 　　5. liquid to solid

Activity 15 (p. 9)
1. from the heater out into the room because it flows from a place of heat concentration to places where there is less heat
2. from the fire to the marshmallow and the air around it because it flows from a place of heat concentration to places where there is less heat
3. from the pizza into the air inside the refrigerator because it flows from a place of heat concentration to places where there is less heat
4. Answers will vary.

Activity 16 (p. 9)
Answers will vary. Teacher check picture.

Activity 17 (p. 10)
Answers will vary. Teacher check picture. Heat does not travel as easily through rubber or plastic as it does through metal, so the handle stays cooler.

Activity 18 (p. 10)
1. white; light colors reflect infrared radiation
2. black; dark colors absorb more infrared radiation

Activity 19 (p. 11)
1. A fan moves air so cool air rushes to take the place of rising warm air and pushes it farther up where it will cool faster and sink back down.
2. There is no air in space.
3. Convection cannot take place without air, and the vacuum trapped between the glass layers contains very little air.
4. Answers will vary.

Activity 20 (p. 11)
1. b 　　2. c 　　3. b 　　4. c

Activity 21 (p. 12)
Answers will vary. Teacher check picture.

Activity 22 (p. 12)
Answers will vary. Teacher check picture.

Activity 23 (p. 13)
1. potential energy 　　2. kinetic energy
3. potential energy 　　4. potential energy
5. potential energy 　　6. kinetic energy

Activity 24 (p. 13)
1. a   2. b   3. a   4. c   5. a

Activity 25 (p. 14)
1. b   2. b   3. a   4. b   5. a

Activity 26 (p. 14)
1. False   2. False   3. False   4. False
5. True   6. True   7. True   8. False

Activity 27 (p. 15)
1. c   2. a   3. e   4. b   5. d

Activity 28 (p. 15)
1. blood: plasma, red cells, white cells, platelets
2. paint: water, pigment (color), binder (glue)
3. smoke: air, ash, carbon monoxide, other gases
4. muddy water: water, silt (fine dirt)
5. fog: air, fine water droplets

Activity 29 (p. 16)
1. c   2. d   3. b   4. e   5. a

Activity 30 (p. 16)
1. solute   2. solvent   3. dissolve
4. solution   5. soluble   6. insoluble

Activity 31 (p. 17)
1. settle   2. evaporates   3. filter
4. distillation   5. centrifuging

Activity 32 (p. 17)
1. suspension, solution, and emulsion
2. filtration, evaporation, distillation, settling, or centrifuging
3. makes substances mix that would not mix otherwise, such as oil and water, by breaking one of the substances into droplets that can be suspended
4. Answers will vary.

Activity 33 (p. 18)
1. table salt   2. citric acid   3. water
4. quartz   5. glass

Activity 34 (p. 18)
1. sugar   2. methane   3. seashells
4. dioxide   5. aspirin

Activity 35 (p. 19)
1. Metals   2. properties   3. shiny
4. reacts   5. electricity   6. solid

Activity 36 (p. 19)
1. not metal   2. metal   3. not metal
4. metal   5. metal

Activity 37 (p. 20)
Metal: aluminum, tin, iron, copper
Not Metal: wood, plastic, helium, glass

Activity 38 (p. 20)
1. iron: frying pans and fence railings
2. silver: coatings for fancy forks, spoons and knives
3. copper: pipes and electrical wiring
4. gold: wedding rings and crowns for teeth
5. lead: shields to protect people from X-rays

Activity 39 (p. 21)
1. brass   2. bronze   3. solder
4. steel   5. stainless steel

Activity 40 (p. 21)
1. alloy   2. iron   3. carbon
4. metal   5. iron, magnets

Activity 41 (p. 22)
1. nitrogen, oxygen, hydrogen   2. carbon
3. sulfur   4. phosphorus   5. selenium

Activity 42 (p. 22)
gases, helium, metals, electricity, solar, elements, chlorine

Activity 43 (p. 23)
1. elements   2. nonmetals   3. metals
4., 5., and 6. (in any order) semimetals, halogens, noble gases

Activity 44 (p. 23)
1. solid   2. molecules   3. structure
4. minerals   5. surfaces   6. faces
7. triangular   8. hexagonal

Activity 45 (p. 24)
1. table salt   2. diamond   3. snow
4. quartz   5. glass

Activity 46 (p. 24)
1. chemical   2. compounds   3. reactants
4. products   5. paper   6. penny
7. copper   8. oxygen

Activity 47 (p. 25)
Chemical Changes: a can rusting, natural gas burning, a penny turning green
Physical Changes: a can being crushed, paper being cut, sugar dissolving in water

Activity 48 (p. 25)
1. citric   2. acetic   3. tannic
4. carbonic   5. ascorbic

Activity 49 (p. 26)
1. milk   2. ammonia   3. toothpaste
4. baking soda   5. soap

Activity 50 (p. 26)
1. blue to red   2. red to blue   3. red to blue
4. blue to red   5. blue to red   6. no change

Activity 51 (p. 27)
Vinegar, alkali, baking soda, neutralize, reaction, chemical, dioxide, atmosphere

Activity 52 (p. 27)
1. acid, fluid, liquid 2. base, fluid, mixture, liquid
3. product, fluid, gas, organic compound
4. fluid, compound 5. solid, metal, alloy, conductor

Activity 53 (p. 28)
1. carbon dioxide   2. burn   3. energy
4. decay   5. material

Activity 54 (p. 28)
animals, sea, layers, rock, oil, Petroleum, cycle, Coal, forests, fossil fuels

Activity 55 (p. 29)
1. silk: cloth made from the cocoons of certain caterpillars
2. wool: cloth made from the fleece of sheep
3. cotton: cloth made from the fuzzy head of a plant
4. linen: cloth made from stems of the flax plant
5. yarn: spun fibers that can be knit or woven into cloth
6. loom: equipment used to weave cloth

Activity 56 (p. 29)
synthetic, rayon, pulp, plant, chemicals, nylon, acrylic, polyester

Activity 57 (p. 30)
1. a   2. b   3. a   4. c   5. a

Activity 58 (p. 30)
1. e   2. g   3. d   4. c   5. b
6. a   7. f

Activity 59 (p. 31)
1. force   2. attracts 3. gravity   4. pencil
5. object   6. mass, gravitational

Activity 60 (p. 31)
1. c   2. a   3. c   4. b   5. b

Activity 61 (p. 32)
1. poles   2. charges   3. south   4. pull
5. push   6. repel   7. attract

Activity 62 (p. 32)
1. magnetic field   2. south pole   3. axis
4. north pole   5. south pole   6. axis
7. north pole   8. magnetic field

Activity 63 (p. 33)
1. fossilized tree sap   2. amber
3. rub it on a piece of fur
4. a feather or anything small and light   5. no

Activity 64 (p. 33)
1. electrostatics   2. charged   3. attract
4. atoms   5. electrons   6. positive
7. negative   8. negative   9. attract

Activity 65 (p. 34)
thunderstorm, charged, ions, Positively, base, electrons, bolt, balancing

Activity 66 (p. 34)
1. b   2. c   3. a   4.c   5. b

Activity 67 (p. 35)
Electrons, electricity, current, flow, metal, atom, plastic, insulator

Activity 68 (p. 35)
1. the flow of electricity through a wire
2. Leopold Nobili
3. in his experiments with resistance and heat
4. the joule, a unit of energy

Activity 69 (p. 36)
1. no   2. negative ions
3. absorbs the extra electrons
4. nickel and cadmium
5. cars, flashlights, cell phones, cameras, etc.

Activity 70 (p. 36)
1. c   2. e   3. d   4. b   5. a

Activity 71 (p. 37)

Activity 72 (p. 37)
1. resistance   2. heat
3. toasters, irons, heaters   4. filament
5. measurement

Activity 73 (p. 38)
1. Hans Christian Oersted
2. Andre Marie Ampere
3. He wrapped a wire around an insulated iron rod.
4. You can turn it on and off.

Activity 74 (p. 38)
1. automobiles   2. aluminum   3. particles
4. Magnetic   5. electromagnets

Activity 75 (p. 39)
1. scientists   2. motion   3. electromagnetism
4. electricity   5. Generators

Activity 76 (p. 39)
1. electricity   2. 1888   3. the rotor   4. taking turns
5. It flows in one direction and then flows in the opposite direction.

Activity 77 (p. 40)
1. oil lamp   2. bicycle   3. garden hose
4. binoculars   5. charcoal grill

Activity 78 (p. 40)
1. c   2. a   3. b   4. c   5. a

Activity 79 (p. 41)
1. f   2. d   3. e   4. b   5. a   6. c

Activity 80 (p. 41)
1. Ohm   2. Ampere   3. Tesla
4. Faraday   5. Franklin

Activity 81 (p. 42)

2. bowler $\xrightarrow[\text{energy}]{\text{work}}$ ball $\longrightarrow$ pins

3. worker $\xrightarrow[\text{energy}]{\text{work}}$ hammer $\longrightarrow$ nail

Activity 82 (p. 42)
1. ax   2. front tooth   3. snowplow
4. chisel   5. nail   6. backrest

Activity 83 (p. 43)
1. wheelchair ramp   2. freeway on-ramp
3. bridge approach   4. moving van loading ramp
5. ship's gangplank

Activity 84 (p. 43)
1. Ferris wheel   2. waterwheel
3. steering wheel   4. fan   5. spinning wheel

Activity 85 (p. 44)
1. doorknob   2. skateboard
3. bike   4. rolling suitcase

Activity 86 (p. 44)
1. spiral staircase   2. bolt   3. corkscrew
4. jar lid thread   5. drill bit   6. lightbulb end

Activity 87 (p. 45)
Not Levers: ax, on-ramp, bicycle wheel, garden hose end, screw, nail, nose, ear, candle
Levers (in any order) seesaw, bicycle hand brakes, wheelbarrow, bottle opener, toilet handle, nail clipper, stapler, arm, tongs, tweezers

Activity 88 (p. 45)
Answers will vary. Teacher check pictures.

Activity 89 (p. 46)
1. turning point   2. fulcrum   3. wrench
4. bolt   5. hinge

Activity 90 (p. 46)
raise, pulley, load, energy, distance, pull, force, machine, crane

Activity 91 (p. 47)
Simple Machine: switchback on a trail, rolling pin, spiral staircase
Complex Machine: bicycle, backhoe, automobile

Activity 92 (p. 47)
toothed, mesh, beside, transmit, opposite, quickly, easier, distance, effort, clocks

Activity 93 (p. 48)
1. b   2. d   3. e   4. f   5. c   6. a

Activity 94 (p. 48)
1. work   2. machine   3. complex machine
4. fulcrum   5. inclined plane

Activity 95 (p. 49)
vacuum, released, bottom, faster, object, exactly, hammer, same

Activity 96 (p. 49)
Newton, experiments, Laws, Motion, forces, effects

Activity 97 (p. 50)
Answers will vary.

Activity 98 (p. 50)
Answers will vary.

Activity 99 (p. 51)
1. Third, opposite   2. Law   3. action
4. reaction   5. rushing

Activity 100 (p. 51)
1. First Law   2. Third Law   3. Second Law
4. Third Law   5. Second Law   6. First Law
7. Third Law

Activity 101 (p. 52)
1. distance   2. displacement   3. speed
4. velocity   5. acceleration   6. momentum

Activity 102 (p. 52)
1. force   2. heat   3. wear   4. reduce
5. waste   6. slippery 7. rubbing

Activity 103 (p. 53)
1. cars, planes, trains, trucks, or buses (any four)
2. saves fuel, improves top speed, improves control
   in high winds
3. air resistance   4. curves

Activity 104 (p. 53)
Good: allows pencils to write, makes brakes work,
   keeps us from slipping when we walk
Bad: wears out machine parts, wastes energy, causes
   unwanted heat

Activity 105 (p. 54)
1. C   2. C   3. NC 4. NC 5. C

Activity 106 (p. 54)
1. False: he continues to fall at the same rate.
2. False: it continues to fall at the same rate.
3. True
4. False: would be different on every planet and
   moon in the solar system.

Activity 107 (p. 55)
1. a   2. c   3. c   4. a   5. a (c is also correct)

Activity 108 (p. 55)
Elasticity: trampoline, rubber band, stretch material in
   a bathing suit
Plastic Behavior: clay, wet sand, cookie dough

Activity 109 (p. 56)
1. movement   2. pattern   3. frequency
4. amplitude   5. instruments

Activity 110 (p. 56)
1. space   2. Transverse
3. Longitudinal   4. oscillation

Activity 111 (p. 57)
1. light, motion   2. thought experiment
4. lightning   5. ground
6. observers   7. time

Activity 112 (p. 57)
1. inertia   2. light   3. planets
4. sunlight   5. dimensional 6. mass

Activity 113 (p. 58)
1. b   2. c   3. a   4. b   5. c   6. b

Activity 114 (p. 58)
1. c   2. d   3. i   4. a   5. g
6. b   7. h   8. f   9. j   10. e

Activity 115 (p. 59)
1. electromagnetic   2. visible   3. faster
4. waves   5. straight

Activity 116 (p. 59)
1. transverse   2. space   3. vacuum
4. intensity   5. spread

Activity 117 (p. 60)
1. transparent   2. translucent   3. opaque
4. translucent   5. opaque   6. translucent
7. opaque   8. opaque   9. transparent

Activity 118 (p. 60)
Convex: human eye, makes light waves bend inward,
   bulges outward, converging
Concave: makes light waves bend outward, curves
   inward, projector, diverging

Activity 119 (p. 61)
1. wavelengths   2. frequencies   3. beam
4. ruby   5. coherent

Activity 120 (p. 61)
1. matter   2. density   3. slows
4. bent   5. refraction 6. break

Activity 121 (p. 62)
1. microscope 2. telescope   3. magnifying glass
4. prescription eyeglasses   5. binoculars

Activity 122 (p. 62)
1. incident   2. reflected   3. angle   4. regular
5. different   6. diffuse   7. shiny

Activity 123 (p. 63)
1. focus   2. film   3. digital
4. projector   5. concave

Activity 124 (p. 63)
1. wavelengths   2. color   3. white   4. prism
5. violet   6. reflecting   7. except

Activity 125 (p. 64)
1. electromagnetic spectrum   2. infrared
3. ultraviolet
4. gamma rays, X-rays, microwaves, radio waves

Activity 126 (p. 64)
1. shorter   2. sunlight   3. tissues
4. fake   5. insects   6. purification

Activity 127 (p. 65)
1. b   2. c   3. a   4. b   5. a

Activity 128 (p. 65)
1. fire   2. torches   3. fat
4. lanterns   5. bulbs   6. convert

Activity 129 (p. 66)
1. c   2. a   3. c   4. c   5. a   6. b

Activity 130 (p. 66)
1. They are the same length.
2. They are the same length.
3. Both squares are the exact same shade of gray.
4. They aren't.

Activity 131 (p. 67)
1. f   2. d   3. e   4. a
5. c   6. g   7. h   8. b

Activity 132 (p. 67)
1. b   2. c   3. c   4. b   5. b   6. a   7. c

Activity 133 (p. 68)
1. Sound waves cannot travel through a vacuum.
2. by pushing molecules together
3. with a vibrating object
4. They spread outward in all directions from their source.

Activity 134 (p. 68)
1. slowly   2. temperatures   3. water
4. farther   5. speed   6. Thunder

Activity 135 (p. 69)
1. loud   2. intensity   3. loudness   4. source
5. decibels   6. silence   7. Whale   8. ears

Activity 136 (p. 69)
1. earthquake   2. frequency   3. oscillations
4. vibrate   5. ultrasound   6. infrasound
7. dolphins

Activity 137 (p. 70)
1. resonant   2. swing   3. vibrates
4. shatter   5. higher

Activity 138 (p. 70)
1. c   2. a   3. c   4. b   5. c

Activity 139 (p. 71)
1. bounce   2. reflected   3. source
4. echolocation   5. navigation

Activity 140 (p. 71)
1. reflect   2. absorb   3. control
4. traffic   5. soundproofed   6. acoustics

Activity 141 (p. 72)
1. converted   2. sampled   3. digital
4. binary   5. compact   6. listening

Activity 142 (p. 72)
1. b   2. a   3. f   4. g
5. h   6. d   7. e   8. c

Activity 143 (p. 73)
Lighter than air: Joseph and Jacques Montgolfier, helium airship, balloon, blimp,
Heavier than air: Orville and Wilbur Wright, airplane, helicopter, passenger jet

Activity 144 (p. 73)
1. airfoil   2. curved   3. faster   4. pressure
5. denser   6. drag   7. thrust   8. engines

Activity 145 (p. 74)
1. Archimedes   2. bath   3. water
4. fluid   5. displace   6. float

Activity 146 (p. 74)
Floats: a ping-pong ball, a wood pencil, an empty bottle with a lid, a marshmallow
Doesn't Float: a coin, a paper clip, a ball of clay, fingernail clippers

Activity 147 (p. 75)
1. matter   2. indivisible   3. atoms
4. particles   5. properties   6. smallest
7. existence   8. microscope

Activity 148 (p. 75)
1. c   2. d   3. g   4. f   5. b   6. a   7. e

Activity 149 (p. 76)
1. matter   2. element   3. oxygen
4. molecule   5. compound   6. hydrogen
7. water

Activity 150 (p. 76)
Elements: oxygen, hydrogen, nitrogen
Compounds: water, rust, table salt

Activity 151 (p. 77)
compounds, substances, elements, chlorine,
electricity, isolate, Dmitri, chart, predicted, Periodic

Activity 152 (p. 77)
1. element   2. numbers   3. protons
4. Periodic   5. rows   6. similar
7. Groups   8. nonmetals   9. hydrogen

Activity 153 (p. 78)
1. strange   2. uranium   3. radium
4. cancer   5. stable   6. Geiger
7. chemistry

Activity 154 (p. 78)
1. mass   2. energy   3. a large amount
4. The nuclei in stable atoms are bonded more
   powerfully and are harder to split off.
5. The atom bomb, used against Japan.

Activity 155 (p. 79)
1. alpha particles, beta particles, gamma rays
2. penetrating high-speed rays that are part of the
   electromagnetic spectrum released after alpha or
   beta particles are cast off
3. alpha particles   4. at the speed of light

Activity 156 (p. 79)
1. cancer   2. radioactive   3. broken
4. irradiate   5. artifacts

Activity 157 (p. 80)
1. nuclear   2. electricity   3. fission
4. unstable   5. fusion   6. waste

Activity 158 (p. 80)
1. c   2. d   3. b   4. a   5. f   6. g   7. e

Activity 159 (p. 81)
Renewable: geothermal, solar, wind, tidal, hydroelectric
Nonrenewable: coal, oil, natural gas

Activity 160 (p. 81)
1. limited   2. aluminum   3. resources
4. energy   5. steel   6. plastic

Activity 161 (p. 82)
Answers will vary.

Activity 162 (p. 82)
1. Newton   2. Einstein   3. Curie
4. Tesla   5. Galileo

Activity 163 (p. 83)
1. hydrogen   2. robotics   3. nanomotors
4. virtual reality
5. light emitting diodes
6. cheap wind-up laptops

Activity 164 (p. 83)
1. f   2. e   3. a   4. h   5. g
6. i   7. b   8. c   9. d

Activity 165 (p. 84)
1. g   2. d   3. h   4. f
5. a   6. c   7. b   8. e

Activity 166 (p. 84)
1. i   2. e   3. f   4. a   5. g
6. h   7. b   8. d   9. c